CORRECTION MARKS FOR PART II
PUNCTUATION

MARK	FAULT	SECTION
⟩	Comma needed	*1*
n – ⟩	Unnecessary comma	*2*
⸴	Error in use of semicolon	*3*
⫶	Error in use of colon	*4*
·	Error in use of period	*5*
?	Error in use of question mark	*6*
/	Error in use of exclamation mark	*7*
—	Error in use of dash	*8*
( )	Error in use of parentheses	*9*
[ ]	Error in use of brackets	*10*
· · ·	Error in use of ellipsis marks	*11*

THE ESSENTIAL ENGLISH HANDBOOK AND RHETORIC

C. Jeriel Howard
Northeastern Illinois University

Richard Francis Tracz
Oakton Community College

Bobbs-Merrill Educational Publishing
A Publishing Subsidiary of **ITT**
Indianapolis

The Bobbs-Merrill Company, Inc.
4300 West 62nd Street
Indianapolis, Indiana 46268

Acquisitions Editor: Paul E. O'Connell
Editing, Design, and Make-Up:
The Bookmakers, Incorporated, Wilkes-Barre, Pennsylvania

Library of Congress Cataloging in Publication Data

Howard, C. Jeriel, 1939–
    The essential English handbook and rhetoric.

    Includes index.
    1. English language — Grammar — 1950–   . 2. English
language — Rhetoric.   I. Tracz, Richard Francis.
II. Title.
PE1112.H68   1985   808'.042   84–16810
ISBN 0–672–61628–9

First Edition
Printed in the United States of America

	1	2	3	4	5	6	7	8	9	PRINTING
84	85	86	87	88	89	90	91	92	93	YEAR

PART II
PUNCTUATION

PART III
MECHANICS

PART IV
PARAGRAPHS AND ESSAYS

PART V
WRITING RESEARCH PAPERS

PREFACE

Often students, and faculty members as well, ask us
to recommend a short text which they can use for help with
their writing. "We don't want a book of exercises," they say.
"We simply want a quick reference guide that will give us the
essentials of correct usage and provide help in essay
organization and development. We want a book that we can
use in all of our college courses, one clearly organized with
examples to show us what is right and what is wrong."

The Essential English Handbook and Rhetoric is just such a book.
While we have not addressed every problem that students might
face, we have presented the essentials. Part I presents the most
common usage concerns, offers brief, simple explanations, and
provides examples of both correct and incorrect patterns. We
have not included drill exercises. In our combined two decades
of teaching composition, neither of us has ever used the exercises that are a part of traditional handbooks, finding them not
only too closely tied to ineffective miscue analysis but also too
undeveloped to reinforce skill acquisition. Part II is a brief,
process-oriented rhetoric, offering students suggestions for finding and limiting topics, organizing ideas, and rewriting. This
section, too, contains many examples, including a sample
research paper that illustrates both traditional footnote
documentation and the new MLA in-text documentation.

Throughout both parts of *Essential* we have emphasized the
contractual bond between the writer and reader. We stress
that the writer must constantly keep in mind his or her reader
and must not make that reader work unnecessarily to arrive
at the meaning of a sentence, a paragraph, or an essay. The
writer uses punctuation not to make a sentence correct but to

guide the reader in following its syntactic patterns. The writer uses appropriate pronoun cases with precise antecedents so that the reader easily understands who the **he** or **she** is. The writer uses parallelism, not because it is "correct" but because it makes for smoothness and demonstrates parallel thinking as well as parallel writing. And the writer uses effective patterns of essay organization and appropriate transitions between the paragraphs to assist the reader in understanding ideas as they exist in the writer's mind. The writer's task must always be to make the reader's work easy and meaningful.

We are indebted to many people for their help as we planned and developed the text. Our own students contributed greatly during our own prewriting stage; their specific questions and concerns shaped the contents of our package. During the final writing and subsequent rewriting, we were given extremely helpful advice from both high school and college reviewers, several of whom are themselves successful textbook authors. We especially wish to thank the following individuals for their useful suggestions: Jo Ann Bonze, Beaver College; Robert Evans, New Hartford High School, New Hartford, New York; Kathleen W. Lampert, Wayland High School, Wayland, Massachusetts; Ben W. McClelland, Rhode Island College; Susan Sanders, Northern Essex Community College; Robert A. Schwegler, University of Rhode Island; Joyce Sigurdson, Queensborough Community College; and Donald J. Tighe, Valencia Community College. And we thank David Samuels, who gave us permission to use his research paper on John Quincy Adams.

Finally, we thank Pretza and Herr Schmitz who continue to provide unity, coherence, and emphasis for our own lives.

C. Jeriel Howard
Richard Francis Tracz

PART I
THE SENTENCE:
GRAMMAR
AND STYLE

1. THE COMPLETE SENTENCE

Effective writing depends upon a contractual relationship between writer and reader. A successful writer and a perceptive reader must each have a general understanding about how the other works, about what each expects of the other. Some of the terms of the contract can be explained logically; others are, admittedly, arbitrary. If you do not want to violate the terms your reader has agreed to—that is, if you do not want to make your reader do additional work decoding a private new system of writing—then you should work as closely as possible to abide by conventional and expected patterns. Certainly the standard written sentence is one of the most important of these patterns.

The sentence is the basic unit of written discourse. When you think, you do not necessarily think in sentences. You call to mind words or clusters of words that have meaning at the time but use them to communicate only with yourself; only you know your intent and purpose. When you write, you must formalize those thoughts — those words and word clusters — into the convention of the sentence. If you fail to do so, you place an undue burden on your reader, who expects you to communicate within the accepted system.

A standard written sentence is a two-part structure consisting of a *subject-member* and a *predicate-member* and expressing a sense of completeness — a complete thought. The challenge of working with sentences lies in recognizing completeness, not in writing subjects and predicates. When you write, you make a transfer from your own thought processes, probably not in the form of complete sentences, to written discourse, which is by its very nature more formal than private thought. Some of the so-called errors discussed in this unit are the direct result of this thinking–writing process. Because your casual conversation is often made up of sentence fragments — "The way I thought it would be" or "Ready to go" — you may also find yourself writing fragments if you are not careful.

By applying our definition, then, **John ran** is a complete sentence but **John** or **ran** is a fragment:

John   /   **ran.**

subject   predicate

To add detail to your sentences, you can add modifiers to either the subject or the predicate or to both:

My cousin **John** from Milwaukee   /   **ran.**

subject   predicate

John   /   **ran** four miles for the first time yesterday.

subject   predicate

My cousin **John** from Milwaukee /

subject

ran four miles for the first time yesterday.

predicate

Some sentences need a ***direct object*** to complete their meaning. The direct object follows the verb and receives the action contained in the verb:

Alan / **threw** / **the book.**

subject   verb   direct object

Her friend **Alan** angrily **threw the** chemistry **book** down.

Book tells what Alan threw.

Other sentences require a ***subject complement*** to sound complete. Indeed, the subject complement is sometimes called a ***verb completer.***

Alice / **is** / **sick.**

subject   verb   verb completer

Alice, who works in our office, **is sick** today.

Sick modifies Alice by telling **how** she is.

The cake looks fantastic.

The three-layered **cake looks** absolutely **fantastic.**

Fantastic modifies cake by telling **how** it looks.

Verbs that often require completers are ***be-verbs*** (**is, am, are, was, were, will be, become,** and **been**) and ***sense verbs*** (such as **looks, tastes, feels, smells, seems, sounds**).

2. SENTENCE FRAGMENTS

A. OMITTED-SUBJECT FRAGMENTS

Sometimes you understand the subject so well that you fail to include it in your written sentence so that your reader will also know it. At other times, the subject may appear in the previous sentence so that you need to connect the two sentences or repeat the subject for the second.

INCORRECT

Reminded me of my own experiences in high school.

Lack spirit and motivation.

CORRECT

The movie I saw last night reminded me of my own experiences in high school.

The players seem tired tonight, for they lack spirit and motivation.

B. OMITTED-VERB FRAGMENTS

An omitted-verb fragment usually occurs as the second "sentence" in a series. If you find yourself writing such fragments, you can provide this second part with its own verb or, in many instances, attach it to the sentence that comes immediately before it.

INCORRECT

The tremendous quantity of work I am doing at school, at work, and at home.

4

CORRECT

I seem to be unusually tired this semester. The **reason is** the tremendous quantity of work that I am doing at school, at work, and at home.

I seem to be unusually tired this semester **because** of the tremendous quantity of work I am doing at school, at my job, and at home.

C. ADVERB CLAUSE FRAGMENTS

A *clause* is a group of words with a subject and predicate. An *independent clause* can stand alone because it makes sense by itself. It is, by definition, a sentence. A *dependent clause* cannot stand alone; it depends for meaning and completeness upon another clause that appears either before it or after it.

One of the most common clause fragments is the *adverb clause* fragment. Such clauses often appear at the beginnings of sentences, but they should never be punctuated as though they are sentences. Typical signal words for these clauses are **when, because, after, until, although, before,** and **while.** To complete the adverb clause fragment, use a comma to connect it to the independent clause that follows.

INCORRECT

When I first get up in the morning.

Although I have not read the book.

Because he works so well under stress.

CORRECT

When I first get up in the morning, **I don't want to talk to anyone.**

Although I have not read the book, **I understand that *Computers for Everyone* is very informative.**

5

Because he works so well under stress, **Larry has been promoted to assistant manager of the new office.**

You can also correct the adverb clause fragment by moving it to the end of the sentence and placing the independent clause at the beginning.

CORRECT

I don't want to talk to anyone **when I first get up in the morning.**

I understand that *Computers for Everyone* is very informative, **although I have not read the book.**

Larry has been promoted to assistant manager of the new office **because he works so well under stress.**

D. ADJECTIVE CLAUSE FRAGMENTS

Adjective clauses are introduced by these signal words: **who, whom, which, that,** and **whose.** The adjective clause is a dependent clause; it cannot stand alone. It should be placed with an independent clause immediately after the noun it modifies.

INCORRECT

That I received for my birthday present.

Whose sister is a lawyer in Memphis.

CORRECT

Have you seen the new stereo that I received for my birthday?

I want you to meet Gene, whose sister is a lawyer in Memphis.

E. PARTICIPIAL PHRASE FRAGMENTS

The *present participle* is the **verb + ing (seeing, running, speaking).** The *past participle* is the third principal part of the verb **(turned, talked, bought).** A clause introduced by either a present participle or a past participle cannot stand alone. Either an independent clause must come before it or after it, or it must be fused into an existing independent clause.

INCORRECT

Speaking as sternly as possible.

Burned to a crisp.

Lay for a week in the garage.

CORRECT

Speaking as sternly as possible, **Susan argued her case.**

Susan argued her case, speaking as sternly as possible.

Burned to a crisp, **the bacon was awful.**

The bacon, burned to a crisp, **was awful.**

The suit that was stolen lay for a week in the garage.

F. INFINITIVE PHRASE FRAGMENTS

An *infinitive* consists of **to + a verb (to sing, to run, to dance, to laugh).** A clause beginning with an infinitive cannot stand as a sentence. It usually serves as the subject of a sentence (when it comes at the beginning of the sentence) or as the direct object of the verb (when it comes near the end of the sentence).

INCORRECT

To run at least three times a week.

To prepare something special for the party.

CORRECT

To run at least three times a week **helps keep an individual physically fit.**

Eileen wanted to prepare something special for the party.

3. JOINING SENTENCES

A. USING COORDINATING CONJUNCTIONS

And, but, or, nor, for, and **yet** are *coordinating conjunctions.* They can be used to coordinate or combine two sentences of equal importance. Remember that you must have a complete sentence on both sides of the coordinating conjunction. In most instances, you should place a comma after the first sentence, just before the conjunction.

I wanted to go to the football game yesterday, **but** my boss insisted that I work instead.

My goal is to become a CPA, **and** I certainly intend to accomplish that objective.

Did you complete the assignment for biology, **or** are you going to do it tonight?

You may omit the comma in a very short sentence where there is no possibility of confusion.

I went shopping yesterday **and** my uncle went with me.

Connie called the store a third time **but** no one answered.

Joining two sentences with a coordinating conjunction helps your reader see more clearly the relationship between them. It is especially important, then, that you select the correct conjunction, the one that shows the proper relationship of ideas. For instance, do not use **and** if you intend to show contrast; do not use **but** if you want to add to the previous idea.

B. USING THE SEMICOLON

You may join two independent clauses (complete sentences) with a semicolon. Be certain that the clause on each side of the semicolon is a complete sentence itself.

My car is in the shop for a tune-up; I should have it by tomorrow afternoon.

The musicians at last night's concert were fantastic; they played all my favorite songs.

C. USING THE SEMICOLON WITH A CONJUNCTIVE ADVERB

You may join two sentences by using a *conjunctive adverb* **(however, nevertheless, therefore, then, indeed)** and a semicolon. The conjunctive adverb should clarify for the reader the relationship between the two sentences you are joining; you should therefore select the word that best points up that relationship. When you use a conjunctive adverb to join two sentences, place a semicolon before the adverb and a comma after it.

My car is in the shop for a tune-up; **however,** I should have it by tomorrow afternoon.

The musicians at last night's concert were fantastic; **indeed,** they played all my favorite songs.

Do not use a semicolon, either alone or with a conjunctive adverb, if one of your clauses is introduced by a dependent linking word such as **when, after, although, because, who** or **which.** *(See 2C and 2D.)* Remember that such signal words introduce dependent clauses, not independent clauses. Do not punctuate them as complete sentences.

INCORRECT

I cannot go to the party next week; because I have to work.

It is not safe to eat meat; that is not thoroughly cooked.

CORRECT

I cannot go to the party next week because I have to work.

It is not safe to eat meat that is not thoroughly cooked.

4. PROBLEMS IN JOINING SENTENCES

A. COMMA SPLICES

A *comma splice* (sometimes called *comma fault*) occurs when two sentences are joined with only a comma. To correct this fault, you must either add one of the coordinating conjunctions or use a semicolon instead of the comma.

INCORRECT

I hear that the view from the Sears Tower in Chicago is magnificent, I have never seen it.

My father came to this country from Portugal, his family came five years later.

I hear that the view from the Sears Tower in Chicago is magnificent, **but** I have never seen it.

My father came to this country from Portugal; his family came five years later.

B. FUSED AND RUN-ON SENTENCES

A *fused* or *run-on sentence* occurs when you do not use the appropriate punctuation mark or conjunction to separate the independent clauses of a sentence. The resulting construction forces your reader to sort out your clauses to determine your meaning. You can correct the problem by using either correct punctuation or a coordinating conjunction. *(See 3.)*

This is the hottest day I have ever known everyone is sticky and uncomfortable.

During our vacation last summer we planned to go to California but at the last minute our plans changed my father won a free trip for two to Vancouver he and my mother took me with them on that trip it was exciting to visit a new place.

This is the hottest day I have ever known; everyone is sticky and uncomfortable.

During our vacation last summer we planned to go to California, but at the last minute our plans changed; my father won a free trip for two to Vancouver; **therefore**, he and Mother took me with them on that trip. It was exciting to visit a new place.

5. EXCESSIVE COORDINATION

Avoid the temptation to write long sentences simply by stringing together several independent clauses connected by coordinating conjunctions. Such sentences usually become difficult to read because the relationships among the parts are not clear. You can break such long sentences into two or more sentences, or you can subordinate the ideas in one clause to the ideas in another by using appropriate punctuation and conjunctions.

INEFFECTIVE

I went for a job interview yesterday, **but** Ms. Rankin, the supervisor, had been called away by a personal emergency, **and** the secretary did not know when she would be back, **but** I left my name, and I asked that Ms. Rankin call me when she returned.

IMPROVED

When I went for a job interview yesterday, Ms. Rankin, the supervisor, had been called away by a personal emergency. Since the secretary did not know when she would be back, I left my name and asked that Ms. Rankin call me when she returned.

6. EXCESSIVE SUBORDINATION

Just as you should avoid stringing sentences together with excessive coordination, you should also avoid building sentences by tacking together a series of overlapping subordinate clauses. Be especially careful of the tendency to hang a series of adjective clauses on the ends of your sentences.

INEFFECTIVE

Harold received an award **that** he had secretly wanted **which** was given for his attendance record and **which** carried a two-hundred dollar cash gift.

IMPROVED

Harold received a two-hundred-dollar cash gift, an award he had secretly wanted for his perfect attendance record.

7. MISPLACED MODIFIERS

A. MISPLACED ELEMENTS

If you place a word or phrase out of its customary sentence position, you may seriously distort the meaning. As a general rule, a modifier should fall as close as possible to the word or phrase it modifies. A single adjective usually comes just before the noun or pronoun it modifies; an adjective phrase or clause usually comes immediately after the word it modifies.

MISPLACED

The carpenters that had fallen from the roof picked up the sack of nails.

The bottom of my closet is filled with shoes and boxes which look like a junk chamber.

His mother told him to get dressed for school three times.

CORRECTED

The carpenters picked up the sack of nails that had fallen from the roof.

The bottom of my closet, which looks like a junk chamber, is filled with shoes and boxes.

His mother told him three times to get dressed for school.

Place a limiting adverb such as **only** or **just** immediately before the verb it modifies. If you write **I only eat vegetables,** you are suggesting that all you do is eat; you do not read, sleep, talk, play, or do anything else. If you write **I eat only vegetables,** your intended meaning is clear.

MISPLACED

I **just** want exactly the same things that you do.

The repairs to my boat **only** cost $175.

CORRECTED

I want **just** exactly the same things that you do.

The repairs to my boat cost **only** $175.

Although a sentence may make sense no matter where you put the limiting adverb, its meaning may not be what you intend. Examine the way the following sentences change meaning when the limiting adverb is moved.

I **almost** won all the money from the baseball pool.

I won **almost** all the money from the baseball pool.

Margie **just** bought a new blouse to wear to the party.

Margie bought **just** a new blouse to wear to the party.

Margie bought a new blouse **just** to wear to the party.

B. DANGLING PARTICIPLES

The participle *(see 2E)* is always used as an adjective. When a participial phrase occurs at the beginning of a sentence, it **always** modifies the sentence subject. That subject should be the first noun after the participial phrase; otherwise, the phrase will dangle.

DANGLING

Driving much too fast, the car slammed into the bridge.

Lying too long on the beach, the sun burned Susan.

Purchased on sale just last week, I got a real bargain on that sweater.

CORRECTED

Driving much too fast, George slammed his car into the bridge.

Lying too long on the beach, Susan got sunburned.

Purchased on sale just last week, the sweater was a real bargain.

You can also attach a dangling modifier by moving it to an appropriate spot in the sentence or by providing it with its own subject.

The sweater that I purchased last week was a real bargain.

Susan was lying too long on the beach and got sunburned.

C. DANGLING INFINITIVES

In terms of sentence structure, a *dangling infinitive (see 2E)* is exactly the same as a dangling participle. If you place an infinitive phrase at the beginning of a sentence, you must follow it immediately with its subject.

DANGLING

To pass the course, your term paper must be submitted on time.

To answer the telephone courteously, your tone of voice must be carefully controlled.

CORRECTED

To pass the course, you must submit your term paper on time.

To answer the telephone courteously, you must carefully control the tone of your voice.

D. DANGLING GERUNDS

The *gerund* consists of a **verb + ing** when it is used as a noun. A dangling gerund is most often found at the beginning of a sentence when the gerund is preceded by an adverb. You can attach a dangling gerund in the same way you attach a dangling participle or an infinitive: Follow the gerund phrase immediately with its subject.

DANGLING

After **seeing the movie,** all the enthusiastic reviews seemed justified.

Before **returning the library book,** it was lost.

CORRECTED

After **seeing the movie,** I think that all the enthusiastic reviews were justified.

Before **returning the library book,** Gail carried it for a month.

E. SQUINTING MODIFIERS

When a modifier occurs between two words or elements and could modify either, it is called a *squinting modifier.* The reader does not know which word or phrase it is intended to modify. To correct the problem, simply move the modifier so it can apply to only one word or phrase.

SQUINTING

The candidate who was speaking **angrily** asked his opponent to clarify her meaning.

CORRECTED

The candidate who was **angrily** speaking asked his opponent to clarify her meaning.

Angrily, the candidate who was speaking asked his opponent to clarify her meaning.

8. PARALLELISM

Sentence elements (words, phrases, or clauses) that take the same form and function in similar structural patterns within the same sentence are *parallel.* To be effective, the parts of the parallel structure must be truly parallel: They must have similar structural patterns and be of equal importance.

Fishing, hunting, and surfing are his favorite activities. (parallel words)

Fishing at his favorite lake, hunting at the family camp, and surfing along the ragged coast are his favorite activities. (parallel phrases)

No one in the audience really knew why the speaker stopped in the middle of his speech or why he suddenly ran from the platform. (parallel clauses)

When I have done my best, I am happy. When I have failed to do my best, I am depressed. (parallel sentences.)

FAULTY

Melvin likes to swim and playing basketball.

A student should carefully observe the way his instructor conducts an experiment and how the results are recorded.

Ms. Gladden has a talent for playing the piano, cooking gorgeous desserts, and to get along with everyone.

Melvin likes to swim and to play basketball.

A student should carefully observe the way his instructor conducts an experiment and how he records his results.

Ms. Gladden has a talent for playing the piano, cooking gorgeous desserts, and getting along with everyone.

9. LOOSE AND PERIODIC CONSTRUCTIONS

A typical English sentence is a *loose sentence:* The sentence kernel (subject, verb, object or complement) comes first; it is then followed by modifying details. A *periodic sentence* reverses this order and saves one of the kernel elements — subject, verb, object or complement — until the very end. The periodic sentence gets its name because the reader must go all the way to the period to get its full meaning.

The periodic sentence provides a valid stylistic technique that can emphasize a major idea or heighten suspense. You should not overuse it, however, or it will lose its effectiveness. Save it to emphasize major ideas.

LOOSE

Alan did not know that he had won the race until he crossed the line and felt the tape snap against his chest.

Many people are frightened by new materialistic attitudes among college students.

PERIODIC

Not until he crossed the line and felt the tape snap against his chest did Alan know he had won the race.

New materialistic attitudes among college students frighten many people.

New materialistic attitudes among college students leave many people frightened.

10. ACTIVE AND PASSIVE PATTERNS

In an *active voice* sentence, the subject performs the action expressed in the verb; in a *passive voice* sentence, the subject receives the action of the verb. Although you will sometimes want to use the passive voice, most of your sentences should be active. A sentence in active voice is shorter and more vigorous than a sentence in the passive.

ACTIVE

The supervisor hurled the report into the wastebasket.

The tornado destroyed the family's home.

PASSIVE

The report was hurled into the wastebasket by the supervisor.

The family's home was destroyed by the tornado.

If you suddenly switch from one voice to another in the same piece of writing, you will probably violate your contractual obligation *(see 1)* to your reader. Making that reader perform unnecessary mental gymnastics by jumping back and forth from active to passive voice sequences is unfair. Shifts in

19

voice most often occur between sentence halves or in two closely related sequential sentences.

MIXED

To prepare for your cocktail party, set up the bar, put glasses out, and snacks should be made before the guests arrive.

CONSISTENT

To prepare for your cocktail party, set up the bar, put out the glasses, and make snacks before the guests arrive.

11. VERBS

The *verb* is usually the word or group of words in a sentence that tells what the subject does.

The boat **sank** slowly to the bottom of the lake.

The politician **boasted** about his record on tax issues.

In some sentences, the verb describes the condition or state of being of the subject. Although the most common state-of-being verb is the **be-verb** *(see 11E),* verbs describing the basic senses **(tastes, feels, smells)** are also state-of-being verbs.

Suzanne **was** very tired last night.

Suzanne **is** at home today.

Suzanne **feels** much better now.

A. SIMPLE TENSES

Verbs show time. By selecting the correct verb tense and using the appropriate verb form for that tense, you indicate to your reader whether an action is past, present, or future.

Although English has nine different verb tenses, the most commonly used of these are the simple tenses, of which there are three.

Simple Present Tense

The *simple present tense* is probably the form you use most often in speaking and writing. It is used in the following situations:

- to describe an action currently taking place.

   I **see** the mountains very clearly.

- to describe a regularly repeated action.

   My father **drives** eighteen miles to work every day.

   I **see** the mountains from my window every morning.

- to describe units of quantity, quality, and location that are always the same.

   There **are** two pints to a quart.

   It **is** seven blocks from my house to the post office.

   The Empire State Building **is** in New York City.

- to write about literature.

   William Faulkner **describes** the South realistically.

   Hawthorne **uses** names in "Young Goodman Brown" to help achieve characterization.

21

* to describe a future action.

    My sister **graduates** from high school next month.

    The Bears **play** the Cowboys next Sunday.

Perhaps the most frequent error made with the simple present tense is the failure to put an **s** on the verb when the subject is in the third person singular. First person **(I)** and second person **(you)** are not followed by the **s** form of the verb, but all other singular subjects are.

I **sing.**	I **speak.**
You **sing.**	You **speak.**
She **sings.**	He **speaks.**

I **trust** my dentist's opinion.

You **trust** your dentist's opinion.

Manfred **trusts** his dentist's opinion.

Simple Past Tense

Use the *simple past tense* to show an action that has already taken place and is complete. Form the past tense of regular verbs by adding either **d** or **ed** to the verb. Because irregular verbs form the past tense in a variety of ways, you can learn them only by memorizing the most common of them *(see chart in Section 11D)*.

My aunt from Australia **visited** us last month.

The Yankees easily **won** last night's game.

I **was** hurt by his unkind remark.

Simple Future Tense

Use the *simple future tense* to describe an action that will occur in the future. Form the future tense by using either **will** or **shall** with the present tense form of the verb.

Our school **will close** on December 22.

You **will do** your best on the next exam.

I **shall reach** my goal!

B. THE PERFECT TENSES

When used to describe tenses, the word *perfect* means **complete.** You should use the perfect tenses to indicate an action completed before another action. Form these tenses by using helping words with the third principal part (past participle) of the verb.

Present Perfect Tense

Form the *present perfect tense* by using **have** or **has** with the past participle of the verb.

I **have seen** the Grand Canyon already.

Lamar **has voted** in the election.

Past Perfect Tense

Form the *past perfect tense* by using **had** with the past participle of the verb.

Before the president left, I **had asked** him for clarification on the procedure.

The orchestra **had played** for three hours before they stopped.

Notice that the verb action of the perfect tense, **had played,** was complete before the verb action of the simple past tense, **stopped.**

My sister **had wanted** a watch for Christmas, but she got a necklace instead.

She **had wanted** a watch before she **got** a necklace.

Future Perfect Tense

Form the *future perfect tense* by using **will have** or **shall have** with the past participle of the verb. This tense describes an action that will be completed at a definite time in the future.

My teacher **will have posted** grades by next Friday.

The savings account **will have earned** eighty dollars in interest by June 30.

C. PROGRESSIVE TENSES

Use the *progressive tense* when you want to show continuous action, that is, action that **progresses.**

Present Progressive Tense

The *present progressive tense* is often used rather than the simple present to describe an action that is presently going on. You form the tense by using either **am, is,** or **are** with the present participle **(verb + ing)** of the verb.

I **am working** at a second job to pay my bills.

Marilee **is teaching** Spanish this semester.

The biology students **are dissecting** frogs this week.

Past Progressive Tense

The *past progressive tense* describes an action that was taking place when another action occurred. It is formed by using **was** or **were** with the present participle of the verb.

The ship **was sinking** slowly when I first saw it.

The victim **was crying** when the police arrived.

The students **were cheating** when the teacher entered the room.

Future Progressive Tense

The *future progressive* tense describes an action that will be taking place when another action happens. It is formed by using **will be** with the present participle of the verb.

I **will be eating** dinner when you call me.

My father **will** still **be working** at 11 P.M.

When you get to San Francisco, they **will be waiting** for you at the airport.

D. PRINCIPAL PARTS OF VERBS

All English verbs have three *principal parts:* the infinitive (present tense), the past tense, and the past participle. Most English verbs are *regular;* that is, the past and past participle are formed by adding either **d** or **ed** to the infinitive: talk, talk**ed,** talk**ed;** close, clos**ed,** clos**ed.** The past and past participle of *irregular verbs,* however, are quite unpredictable. If you are not familiar with the principal parts of a particular verb, check your dictionary. You will find the principal parts listed immediately after the entry for the verb itself.

perform (per-form) v. -formed, -forming

The past and past participle of **perform** are both **performed;** the present participle is **performing.**

throw (thro) v. threw, thrown, throwing

The past tense form of **throw** is **threw,** and the past participle is **thrown.** The present participle is **throwing.**

You are familiar with the principal parts of a large number of irregular verbs because you use them so often. The chart given here lists principal parts for the most frequently used irregular verbs.

PRINCIPAL PARTS OF IRREGULAR VERBS

Infinitive (Present Tense)	Past Tense	Past Participle
arise	arose	arisen
awake	awaked (awoke)	awaked (awoke)
beat	beat	beaten
become	became	become
begin	began	begun
bend	bent	bent
bet	bet	bet
bite	bit	bitten
blow	blew	blown
break	broke	broken
bring	brought	brought
build	built	built
burst	burst	burst
catch	caught	caught
choose	chose	chosen
come	came	come
cut	cut	cut

PRINCIPAL PARTS OF IRREGULAR VERBS (continued)

Infinitive (Present Tense)	Past Tense	Past Participle
deal	dealt	dealt
dive	dived (dove)	dived
do	did	done
draw	drew	drawn
drink	drank	drunk
drive	drove	driven
drown	drowned*	drowned*
eat	ate	eaten
fall	fell	fallen
fight	fought	fought
fly	flew	flown
forget	forgot	forgotten (forgot)
forgive	forgave	forgiven
freeze	froze	frozen
get	got	got (gotten)
give	gave	given
go	went	gone
grow	grew	grown
keep	kept	kept
know	knew	known
lead	led	led
leave	left	left
lend	lent	lent
let	let	let
loan	loaned*	loaned*
lose	lost	lost

*These two verbs are actually regular, but they are often mistakenly treated as though they were irregular.

PRINCIPAL PARTS OF IRREGULAR VERBS (continued)

Infinitive (Present Tense)	Past Tense	Past Participle
mean	meant	meant
prove	proved	proved (proven)
read	read	read
ride	rode	ridden
ring	rang	rung
run	ran	run
say	said	said
see	saw	seen
sell	sold	sold
send	sent	sent
sew	sewed	sewed (sewn)
shake	shook	shaken
shave	shaved	shaved (shaven)
shrink	shrank (shrunk)	shrunk
show	showed	showed (shown)
sink	sank (sunk)	sunk
speak	spoke	spoken
swim	swam	swum
take	took	taken
teach	taught	taught
tear	tore	torn
tell	told	told
think	thought	thought
throw	threw	thrown
wear	wore	worn
win	won	won
write	wrote	written

E. BE-VERBS

The *be-verb* is the most frequently used English verb; it is also the most irregular, having eight forms. Here are the forms for the simple tense patterns.

PRESENT

I **am**	you **are**	he/she/it **is**
we **are**	you **were**	they **are**

PAST

I **was**	you **were**	he/she/it **was**
We **were**	you **were**	they **were**

FUTURE

(all subjects) **will be** or **shall be**

The forms for the perfect tense are **have (has) been** for the present perfect, **had been** for the past perfect, and **will (shall) have been** for the future perfect.

You should avoid overusing the **be-verb** in your writing. It lacks the impact of a more specific verb that might help convey your meaning more effectively.

Harry is the owner of a collection of artwork.

Harry collects artwork.

The first sentence uses three times as many words to say the same thing.

Dependence on too many be-verbs is also likely to cast too many of your sentences into the passive voice *(see 10)*. The passive voice is lengthier and usually less effective than the active.

The car **was wrecked** by Kevin. (passive)

Kevin **wrecked** the car. (active)

F. PROBLEM VERB SETS

Certain English verbs are part of a problem set: two words that sound very much alike but have very different uses.

Lie–Lay

To lie means to rest or recline; it never takes a direct object. *To lay* means to place or put; and always requires a direct object. Here are their principal parts:

Infinitive (Present)	Past	Past Participle	Present Participle
lie	lay	lain	lying
lay	laid	laid	laying

Remember that **lie** never takes a direct object. It simply defines an act of resting or reclining.

My sister likes **lying** on the beach all morning.

I just **lay** around the house all day yesterday.

Lay always requires a direct object. Something is being placed or put somewhere.

Dr. Schwartz could not remember where he **had laid** his stethoscope.

I **will lay** the shirts on the front seat of your car.

Sit–Set

Sit means to be seated; it never takes a direct object. **Set** means to place something in a place or location; it always (like **lay**) requires a direct object. Here are the principal parts:

Infinitive (Present)	Past	Past Participle	Present Participle
sit	sat	sat	sitting
set	set	set	setting

Remember that **sit** never takes a direct object; it simply defines the act of being seated.

I always **sit** near the front of the classroom.

We **were sitting** too close to the screen to see the movie.

Set always takes a direct object; something has to be placed into position or location.

Christopher **set** the flowers on top of the table.

Do you remember where you **set** the dictionary?

Rise – Raise

Rise means to get up; it never takes a direct object. **Raise** means to lift something; it always requires a direct object. Here are the principal parts:

Infinitive (Present)	Past Participle	Past Participle	Present Participle
rise	rose	risen	rising
raise	raised	raised	raising

Remember that **rise** never takes a direct object; it describes the act of getting up.

The crowd **rose** to its feet in excitement.

The judge **had risen** from his chair to address the court.

Raise always takes a direct object; something has to be lifted.

If you know the answer, **raise** your hand.

The crowd **was raising** the flag above the embassy.

G. TENSE CONSISTENCY

Remember your obligation to the reader. If your reader begins to read a passage written in the present tense, he or she will probably be jarred if you suddenly shift to the past tense. You should never shift tenses unnecessarily. Maintaining consistency in tense throughout a given piece of writing is one way in which you can provide the coherence and cohesion that make it easy for your reader to follow what you are trying to express.

TENSE SHIFT

The race car **came** slowly out of the turn; then suddenly it **picks** up speed for the straightaway.

My father **is feeling** sick today, but he **said** he will go to work anyway.

The basketball team **had practiced** its drills and **is** ready for the season's big game.

TENSE CONSISTENCY

The race car **came** slowly out of the turn; then suddenly it **picked** up speed for the straightaway.

My father **is feeling** sick today, but he **says** he will go to work anyway.

The basketball team **had practiced** its drills and **was** ready for the season's big game.

Although it makes sense to maintain tense consistency, this does not mean that you should necessarily use only one tense throughout a piece of writing. It means that you should not change tenses without cause. Look at the following sentence:

My mother **says** that when she was a child her aunt really **spoiled** her.

This sentence has two verb tenses, one present and one past, each describing a different action. A paragraph developed from this sentence would use the present tense to relate everything the mother says and the past tense to describe the aunt's actions in the past.

My mother says that when she was a child her aunt really spoiled her. Mother's favorite story tells what happened when she lost her favorite doll. Her aunt drove her twenty-five miles into town to buy a new one. She says that one time her aunt took her shopping and bought her seven new dresses. And that was during the depression. Even today, Mother remembers how she liked to spend weekends at her aunt's house. She was given her own bedroom and was even served breakfast in bed. She tells me that she used to cry every Sunday night when it was time to return to her own home.

12. SUBJECT AND VERB AGREEMENT

In the present tense, a verb is either singular or plural. The be-verb also changes forms in the past tense for singular and plural. When you write in the present tense, you should always use a singular verb with a singular subject and a plural verb with a plural subject.

If you keep in mind the following basic guidelines, you will solve many of your problems with subject-verb agreement:

- An **s** ending added to a noun usually makes it plural, but that same **s** ending added to a verb makes it singular.

  The new **students ask** a lot of questions. (plural)

  The new **student asks** a lot of questions. (singular)

- Although it is singular, the subject **I** does not require a verb form ending with **s.**

  I sing loudly while taking my morning shower.

- The subject **you** always requires a plural verb form.

  You take the book home with you this weekend.

- It is unusual for both the subject and the verb to end with **s.** An exception occurs when one of the words (usually a proper name) ends in **s.**

  Charles studies for at least three hours every day.

A. SUBJECTS JOINED BY *AND*

Subjects joined by **and** require a plural verb.

INCORRECT

My **aunt** and **uncle is** in town for the homecoming game.

Swimming and **hiking takes** up most of my spare time.

CORRECT

My **aunt** and **uncle are** in town for the homecoming game.
Swimming and **hiking take** up most of my spare time.

The exception to this rule occurs when **each** or **every** comes before the compound subject. These words indicate members of a group considered as individuals; therefore, they require a singular verb.

INCORRECT

Each student and **teacher are** responsible for school morale.

Every member of the football team and his **date are** invited to the special dance next Saturday night.

CORRECT

Each student and **teacher are** responsible for school morale.

Every member of the football team and his **date is** invited to the special dance next Saturday night.

B. SUBJECTS JOINED BY *OR* OR *NOR*

When subjects are joined by **or** or **nor,** the verb should agree in number with the subject closest to it.

INCORRECT

Either the **patient or** the **doctors** is guilty of filing a false insurance claim.

Neither the **doctors nor** the **patient are** guilty of filing a false insurance claim.

Bob or his **cousins** always **picks** up the evening paper.

CORRECT

Either the **patient or** the **doctors** are guilty of filing a false insurance claim.

Neither the **doctors nor** the **patient** is guilty of filing a false insurance claim.

Bob or his **cousins** always **pick** up the evening paper.

C. SUBJECTS WITH FORMS OF *ONE* OR *BODY*

Subjects ending with **one (everyone, no one, anyone)** or **body (everybody, nobody, anybody)** are always singular.

INCORRECT

No one answer the telephone at that extension.

Everybody want to be part of a winning team.

Nobody were able to do the assignment on time.

CORRECT

No one answers the telephone at that extension.

Everybody wants to be part of a winning team.

Nobody was able to do the assignment on time.

D. SUBJECTS WITH INTERRUPTING PATTERNS

Be certain that you identify the true subject of your verb. Some sentences contain *interrupting patterns,* often prepositional phrases, between the true subject and the verb. Do not confuse a noun in that interrupting pattern with the subject of the verb.

INCORRECT

One of the students **are** talking in an abusive manner.

Each of the players **take** a turn at batting practice.

CORRECT

One of the students **is** talking in an abusive manner.

Each of the players **takes** a turn at batting practice.

Be careful with sentences that contain phrases such as **along with, as well as, in addition to, together with,** or **not to mention** after the subject. These phrases do **not** change the number of the true subject.

INCORRECT

My **boss** as well as his wife **are** out of town for a vacation.

The **professor** together with seven of his students **are waiting** to see the dean.

CORRECT

My boss as well as his wife **is** out of town for a vacation.

The **professor** together with seven of his students **is** waiting to see the dean.

E. INVERTED ORDER

In most English sentences, the subject comes before the verb. In some patterns, however, the subject comes after the verb. These patterns appear in clauses introduced by **here** or **there** and in questions. Be certain in those patterns to locate the true subject after the verb.

INCORRECT

Here **are** the **report** that you requested.

There, on the table where everyone could see, **were** the highly secret **document.**

Are everyone planning to go to the conference in Cincinnati?

CORRECT

Here **is** the **report** that you requested.

There, on the table where everyone could see, **was** the highly secret **document.**

Is everyone planning to go to the conference in Cincinnati?

F. COLLECTIVE NOUNS

A *collective noun* is one that refers to a unit made up of several members: for example, **family, jury, committee.** If the collective noun refers to the group acting as a single unit, it requires a singular verb. If the noun refers to individuals or parts operating separately within the larger unit, it requires a plural verb.

INCORRECT

Every **family have** its own traditions.

The **class are** taking a trip to the museum today.

The **majority is** opposed to the amendment being discussed.

CORRECT

Every **family has** its own traditions.

The **class is** taking a trip to the museum today.

The **majority are** opposed to the amendment being discussed.

G. RELATIVE PRONOUNS

A *relative pronoun* (**who, that, which**) takes the same number as the word to which it refers (its antecedent), and the verb must agree in number with that antecedent.

INCORRECT

Among the students, Michael is the only **one** who **are** eager for class to begin.

The **jobs** which **has** been advertised are being filled quickly.

Pretza is the only **one** of the dogs that **are** always sleeping.

CORRECT

Among the students, Michael is the only **one** who **is** eager for class to begin.

The **jobs** which **have** been advertised are being filled quickly.

Pretza is the only **one** of the dogs that **is** always sleeping.

H. SUBJECT AND LINKING VERB

A *linking verb* is so named because it links the subject with another word needed for completion of the idea (called a *subject complement*). The linking verb agrees with the subject, not with the complement.

INCORRECT

Her greatest **concern are** the three tests on Monday.

The three **tests** on Monday **is** her greatest concern.

CORRECT

Her greatest **concern is** the three tests on Monday.

The three **tests** on Monday **are** her greatest concern.

I. TITLES

Titles of books, movies, poems, and plays are singular.

INCORRECT

The Boys from Syracuse **were** actually a musical about ancient Greece.

"The Marshes of Glynn" **are** probably Sidney Lanier's best known poem.

CORRECT

The Boys from Syracuse **was** actually a musical about ancient Greece.

"The Marshes of Glynn" **is** probably Sidney Lanier's best known poem.

13. PRONOUNS

A **pronoun** takes the place of a noun; it is used in writing or speaking to avoid the monotony of repeating the noun again and again. Instead of writing **My father talked with Mary, and Mary said that the briefcase was definitely Mary's,** you would probably write **My father talked with Mary, and she said that the briefcase was definitely hers.** A pronoun can be used only to refer to an *antecedent,* the noun to which the pronoun refers.

A pronoun may be either singular or plural, and it may be any one of three cases: subjective, objective, or possessive. Here is a chart of the case forms.

	First Person	Second Person	Third Person
Subjective Case			
Singular	I	you	he, she, it, who
Plural	we	you	they, who
Objective Case			
Singular	me	you	him, her, it, whom
Plural	us	you	them, whom

	First Person	Second Person	Third Person
Possessive Case			
Singular	my (mine)	your (yours)	his, her (hers), its, whose
Plural	our (ours)	your (yours)	their (theirs), whose

A. SUBJECTIVE CASE USES

The subjective case is used in the following instances:

Subject of a Sentence

You can go in to see Ms. Crawford now.

We are already making plans for an exciting vacation.

Subject Complement

It was **she** who called you yesterday morning.

The surprise speaker for the meeting was **he.**

Subject of a Clause

The supervisor talked with the secretary **who** took the call.

Did you know **he** came to visit me last weekend?

Appositive to Identify the Subject

The two of them, **he** and his pianist, entertained beautifully.

Someone, **she** or her secretary, quoted the wrong price.

B. OBJECTIVE CASE USES

The objective case is used in the following instances:

Direct Object

George's father complimented **him** on his high grades.

I believe that the teacher likes **her** best of all.

Indirect Object

Dr. Allen handed **me** the report.

The payroll office mailed **her** a check just last week.

Object of a Preposition

This is a secret between you and **me.**

Did Lawrence send the report to Arthur or **you?**

Subject of an Infinitive (To + Verb)

The contractor wanted **me** to do the work for him.

The professor asked **us** to review our notes carefully.

Object of an Infinitive

I want you to ask **her** about the weather in Denver.

My brother tried to wrestle **me** to the ground.

Object of a Participle (Verb + ing)

Paying **him** no attention, the clerk continued to talk on the phone.

Telling **us** to speak more slowly, our speech teacher demonstrated the technique.

C. POSSESSIVE CASE USES

The possessive case is used in the following instances:

Ownership or Possession

Gloria found **her** purse at the bottom of the locker.

Your notebook is lying on the dresser.

Subject of a Gerund (Verb + ing)

The man objected to **my** talking so loudly.

Your asking so many questions proved worthwhile.

Be careful not to confuse the gerund with the participle. The gerund has the same form as the present participle, but it is always used as a noun. The participle is always an adjective. Use the possessive case with the gerund, but use the objective case with the participle. As a handy guide, remember that a gerund is the subject generally of a sentence or the object of a preposition that follows a pronoun.

PARTICIPLE

Greg saw **them** taking the money from the drawer.

I heard **you** playing the piano.

43

GERUND

No one approved of **their** taking the money from the drawer.

I enjoyed listening to **your** playing the piano.

Your playing the piano was appreciated.

Subject of a Sentence

Yours will be ready late this afternoon.

Theirs cannot be found anywhere.

Complement

The pair of brown gloves is **mine.**

The keys you found are **hers.**

D. COMPOUND CONSTRUCTIONS

Most errors in case with pronouns occur in compound construc-
tions like **LaVerne and me** or **Roger and she.** Remember that
the presence of another noun in compound with the pronoun
does not change the case of the pronoun that is needed.

INCORRECT

My brother and **me** went to the game last night.

The envelope came addressed to Larry and **I.**

CORRECT

My brother and **I** went to the game last night.

The envelope came addressed to Larry and **me.**

E. AGREEMENT WITH ANTECEDENT

A pronoun must agree with its *antecedent* (the specific word to which it refers) in number. If you use a singular antecedent, you must use a singular pronoun; if your antecedent is plural, use a plural pronoun.

INCORRECT

Everyone believed that **they** should pass the course.

The artist could not find **their** brushes and paint.

Do the page proofs look the way you expected **it** to?

CORRECT

Everyone believed that **he** (or **she**) should pass the course.

The artist could not find **her or his** brushes and paint.

Do the page proofs look the way you expected **them** to?

A pronoun must also agree with its antecedent in person. You should not needlessly shift from one person to another. The most common mistake here is a careless shift to the second person.

INCORRECT

One spends a lot of time sleeping during **your vacation.**

We all went shopping yesterday; **you** really got some bargains at the gigantic sale.

CORRECT

One spends a lot of time sleeping during **his** (or **her**) vacation.

You spend a lot of time sleeping during **your** vacation.

We all went shopping yesterday; **we** really got some bargains at the gigantic sale.

F. CONSISTENCY IN WRITING

It is not sufficient that your pronouns be consistent in number and person within the same sentence; they must also be consistent throughout an entire piece of writing. If you are careless when you write a larger piece, you are likely to find yourself unnecessarily shifting either number or person. If you lead your reader to expect a passage written in the third person singular, you have an obligation not to confuse him or her by suddenly shifting into first person plural for no good reason.

Both the number and the person of a piece of writing are usually indicated in the first or second sentence. As you edit your own work, decide which number and person you intend to use; then be consistent throughout the entire paragraph or essay.

INCONSISTENT

My hobby is collecting records. This is something that **I** have been doing for at least six years. **You** can find a lot of interesting albums, if **you** browse around old record stores and book stores. **I** spend at least four or five hours a week doing just that, but **you** have to be careful to avoid buying damaged records. A **person** looks at **it** very carefully to see that there are no scratches on the surface; sometimes **he** may even get to play **it** before buying **it**. **I** have bought more than three hundred albums and got only about a dozen bad ones. Some of **your** best finds, however, are those **you** discover by trading albums with other collectors. **I** belong to three record exchange groups and get a lot of records from **it**.

CONSISTENT

My hobby is collecting records. This is something that I have been doing for at least six years. I can find a lot of interesting albums if I browse around old record stores and book stores. I spend at least four or five hours a week doing just that, but I have to be careful to avoid buying damaged records. I look at **them** very carefully to see that there are no scratches on **their** surfaces; sometimes I may even get to play **them** before buying them. I have bought more than three hundred albums and got only about a dozen bad ones. Some of **my** best finds, however, are those I discover by trading albums with other collectors. I belong to three record exchange groups and get a lot of records from **them.**

14. WORD CHOICE

A critic once asked Ernest Hemingway to identify the single most difficult task he faced as a writer. After thinking about the question for a while, the famous writer replied that his most difficult task was "finding the right word for the right place."

Indeed, finding the right word is a demanding task. No matter how well you have thought out your ideas and organized them, if you do not use appropriate *diction* (the choice of words for the expression of ideas), your reader will not get the full impact of your message. Using the first word that comes to your mind as you write is often ineffective. Learn to isolate the words in your writing; look at them individually; determine if they are really the right ones, in every instance, to convey your intended meaning.

A. SPECIFIC DICTION

In most instances, you should use specific words rather than general words in your writing.

GENERAL	SPECIFIC
bird	golden eagle
car	1975 Buick
building	Sears Tower
teacher	Mrs. Powers
game	soccer
tool	thin-nosed pliers

Avoid the excessive use of vague, general words that fail to lend precision to your writing. Among the most frequently used vague or general words are these:

fine	thing	item	nice	pretty
instance	interesting	factor	swell	item

VAGUE

Their wedding was very **nice.**

SPECIFIC

Their wedding was a **beautiful** and **emotionally moving** occasion.

B. CONNOTATION AND DENOTATION

Denotation is the dictionary meaning of a word; **connotation** is the emotional meaning of a word. All words have denotative meanings, and many words also have connotative meanings. Good writers learn to use the connotative meanings of the words they use to carry much of the weight of the communication task.

DENOTATIVE	CONNOTATIVE
dog	puppy, mutt
car	limousine, rattle trap

DENOTATIVE	CONNOTATIVE
walk	hobble, saunter
speak	mumble, scream
person	friend, enemy

DENOTATIVE

My uncle says he will rent a **car** to take us to the dance.

The young man **walked** across campus.

The reader knows nothing other than that the young man moved across campus.

CONNOTATIVE

My uncle says he will rent a **limousine** to take us to the dance.

The young man **sailed** across campus. The young man **hobbled** across campus. The young man **dragged** himself across campus.

Each of these sentences conveys something, either positive or negative, about the young man and how he moved across campus.

C. IDIOMS

An *idiom* is an accepted word or phrase which, although it may very well violate principles of grammar or logic, is sanctioned by current usage. In your writing, you should be careful to use the correct idiomatic form. If you are uncertain which preposition to use in a given situation, check your dictionary. There you will find, for instance, that **according** is followed by **to,** meaning the correct idiomatic expression is **according to** and not **according with.** Here is a list of some of the most frequently used idiomatic expressions, along with the unidiomatic forms that are sometimes incorrectly used.

IDIOMATIC	UNIDIOMATIC
according to	according with
acquitted of	acquitted with
adverse to	adverse against
aim to prove	aim at proving
aloud	out loud
as far as	all the farther
angry with	angry at
attend to	tend to
blame me for it	blame it on me
cannot help talking	cannot help but talk
comply with	comply to
conform to/with	conform in
convince that	convince to
desire to	desire of
die of (a disease)	die with
different from	different than
doubt whether/that	doubt if
free from	free of
frightened by/at	frightened of
must	have got to
identical with	identical to
in accordance with	in accordance to
in search of	in search for
kind of	kind of a
listen to	listen at
monopoly of	monopoly for/on
oblivious of	oblivious to
plan to go	plan on going
provided	providing
sensitive to	sensitive about
superior to	superior than
try to	try and
unequal to	unequal for
unmindful of	unmindful about

D. SLANG AND JARGON

Slang words, although currently popular, suggest a casual, forced, racy, vulgar, or offbeat meaning. They may be used in informal oral communication, but they seldom have a place in more structured written communication. A major problem with slang words is that they are ephemeral (do you recall ever hearing anyone say "23 skidoo," a popular slang term of the 1920s?) or they are meaningful only to a closed group (your friends might understand what you mean saying "Last night's concert was a bust," but would your grandmother?)

Slang words come and go so quickly that a list of them is not especially helpful. If you want to write standard, acceptable English, make it a practice to avoid words that are currently the "in" words. They are probably slang. When in doubt, check your choices in a good dictionary and be directed by the label it assigns to the word.

SLANG

The dance last night was really **cool.**

STANDARD

The dance last night was **perfect.**

Jargon is language peculiar to a particular group. Virtually every profession — medicine, law, education, accounting — has its own jargon. Although jargon may be useful to members of the group, it becomes clumsy, wordy, or meaningless to others. Look at the following examples of jargon:

First, you have to **boot up** the system.

Used by an instructor to tell students how to make a computer system operative.

Eileen is an **exceptional** student.

Used by an educator to indicate that Eileen is in a class for slow learners.

The **unfavorable climatic conditions** make it necessary for me to **abort** our flight plans.

Used by an airline pilot to discuss the effect of bad weather.

We cannot pursue matters further until the **parties of the instance** are willing to **meet at the negotiating table.**

Used by a lawyer to explain that the case is at a standstill.

E. CLICHÉS

A cliché is an overworked stock expression that carries very little meaning. Using clichés is an indication of off-top-of-the-head thinking and results in shallow writing. No one — not you and not your reader — has to think about what that cluster of words means.

There are literally hundreds of clichés in our language, and you know most of them already. As you are writing, you will find it a good rule to avoid using clusters of words that pop suddenly into your mind. Chances are rather good that such word clusters are clichés. Here are some samples:

wise as an owl
sharp as a tack
dry as a bone
between a rock and a hard place
a stitch in time saves nine
the early bird gets the worm
early to bed, early to rise
out of the frying pan and into the fire

F. REDUNDANCIES

Redundancy in writing means unnecessarily saying the same thing twice. If your writing is redundant, you are probably not paying attention to the meaning of the words you use. You should correct redundant sequences by eliminating the needless repetition.

REDUNDANT	CONCISE
at 7 A.M. in the morning	at 7 A.M.
twelve o'clock midnight	midnight
advance forward	advance
talked orally	talked
past history	history
new innovation	innovation
blend together with	blend with
visible to the eye	visible
audible to the ear	audible

G. WORDINESS

Wordiness, like redundancy, makes your reader do unnecessary work by reading words or phrases that add no meaning. Many stock expressions which have crept into our language are much more effectively reduced to a single word or a shorter phrase.

WORDY	CONCISE
at this point in time	now
for the purpose of beginning	to begin
in reference to	regarding
due to the fact that	because
in the vicinity of	near

53

WORDY	CONCISE
in many instances	often
in a similar fashion	similarly
throughout the entire day	throughout the day

Wordiness often results from the excessive use of such intensifiers as **very, really, simply, terribly, happy, joyous,** and many others. Although these words are sometimes needed to intensify your meaning, using them unnecessarily makes your writing much less forceful.

WORDY

It was **really** the best gift that I received.

Eric worked **very** hard at his job.

CONCISE

It was the best gift that I had received.

Eric worked hard at his job.

H. CONFUSED PAIRS

Some words sound alike or very nearly alike but actually have very different meanings. For instance, **accept** and **except, compliment** and **complement,** and many other word pairs are widely different in meaning. You should make certain you are using the specific word you need to convey the appropriate meaning. If necessary, use your dictionary to check your accuracy. A list of some of the most frequently confused pairs of words, along with brief definitions, appears in the spelling section of this text *(III 7E).*

I. LEVELS OF DICTION

The diction you choose for a piece of writing should be determined by the components of the rhetorical context: the audience, the purpose, and the occasion. You write (and speak) one way to your cousin in another city and different way to your employer, minister, priest, or rabbi. If your purpose is to tell someone how much fun you had on your vacation, you will use language different from the language you would use to ask for a raise. You would certainly use one level of language at a picnic and a different level at a religious service.

Any level of diction you use will fall into one of the following three categories: standard, informal, and colloquial. Standard diction is most often used in business, industry, and academia. It is the language of business letters, reports, documents, and business meetings. Informal diction is the language you use when you know your audience personally and when your communication is going to be shared with no one else. You might use informal diction to write a brief note to your supervisor asking for next Tuesday off, and you use informal diction in talking with co-workers and friends. In fact, informal diction is more often used in speaking than in writing. Colloquial diction is the language used in only the most casual of situations. It occurs almost always in talking and seldom in writing. You probably employ colloquial diction with your friends in the school cafeteria, at sports events, or at the corner bar. You might write a letter to your cousin or to a close friend in colloquial language.

Here are some words arranged to illustrate the three levels of diction.

STANDARD	INFORMAL	COLLOQUIAL
television	tv	tube
police officer	cop	fuzz
ineffectual	weak	wimpy
demeanor	attitude	looks
disparage	belittle	knock
inefficient	failure	dud
money	cash	bread
talk	chat	rap

Remember that there is nothing either right or wrong about any of these words. Your use of any one of them should depend on your audience, purpose, and occasion. You can make the tone of your writing extremely confusing, however, if you mix levels in the same piece of writing.

INCONSISTENT

The police officer busted the dude for beating up on his old lady.

I simply do not have the bread to make the downpayment for a new car.

The instructor's presentation of the personal strategies for survival during a nuclear disaster was really cool.

CONSISTENT

The police officer arrested the man for assaulting his girl friend.

The cop busted the dude for beating up on his old lady.

I simply do not have the money to make the downpayment for a new car.

The instructor's presentation of the personal strategies for survival during a nuclear disaster was excellent.

PART II
PUNCTUATION

Proper punctuation helps the reader to understand your intended meaning. Marks of punctuation tell that reader to slow down, to connect certain ideas with others, to separate some ideas from others, to comprehend the relationship among the clauses and sentences. Punctuation marks, then, serve the reader in much the same way that highway signs serve the traveler: they provide direction and guidance along the way.

1. THE COMMA

A. BETWEEN INDEPENDENT CLAUSES

Use a comma before a coordinating conjunction to separate two independent clauses. The coordinating conjunctions are **and, but, or, nor, for, so,** and **yet.**

She paged Mr. Gilliam, but he did not respond.

The voters of our city have never taken their task lightly, nor have the politicians ignored the voters' common concerns.

If the two independent clauses are very short, and especially if both clauses have the same subject, you may omit the comma; but it is never wrong to include it. Either of the following sentences is correct.

I am going to bed early tonight, but I will call you first.

I am going to bed early tonight but I will call you first.

You should never omit the coordinating conjunction and use only the comma.

INCORRECT

My father is taking night courses, he continues to work full time at his job.

CORRECT

My father is taking night courses, yet he continues to work full time at his job.

B. TO SEPARATE ITEMS IN A SERIES

Use commas to separate the items in a series from each other. Remember that items in a series may be words, phrases, or clauses.

My favorite junk foods are pizza, hot dogs, hamburgers, and pretzels.

Be certain to bring the following items to camp with you: bedding, night clothes, towels, swim suit, and hiking clothes.

His work is as well done as any I've seen, as professionally marketed as any I know, and as inexpensive as any I've found.

The comma is sometimes omitted before the conjunction if there is no possibility of misreading the sentence. However, it is never incorrect to include it, and making a practice of including it will prevent your writing a sentence that could be misread. Look at this example:

Gene, Gregory and Christine stopped by to visit me yesterday.

This sentence could be addressed to Gene, telling him that Gregory and Christine visited. Or the writer might have meant that all three persons visited yesterday. If so, the meaning would be much clearer if a comma appeared before the conjunction:

Gene, Gregory, and Christine stopped by to visit me yesterday.

C. AFTER INTRODUCTORY WORDS, PHRASES, AND CLAUSES

Use a comma to separate introductory words from the rest of the sentence.

There, I hope you are satisfied now.

Yes, I am looking forward to going with you to Canada.

Well, what did you expect?

Use a comma to separate transitional words or phrases from the rest of the sentence.

Finally, you trust that they will make the right decision.

Accordingly, I am sending you my request for a refund.

In fact, I find the ideas in your report stimulating.

However, the settlement you offer is less than I am willing to accept.

Use a comma to separate long introductory phrases from the rest of the sentence.

After waiting three months for a response to her order, Mrs. Schultz finally bought the fan from another company.

In the poorly lighted back corner of the gym, the boxers continued their workouts.

While waiting for the bus to come, Carlos read his history assignment.

Use a comma to separate an introductory clause from the rest of the sentence.

Before I go to work in the morning, I always read the paper.

Although Michelle enjoys cooking, she dislikes entertaining.

If you are unable to attend the meeting, please call me to let me know.

D. BETWEEN COORDINATE ADJECTIVES

Use a comma to separate coordinate adjectives when they are not separated by a coordinating conjunction. *Coordinate adjectives* are those which modify the same noun equally. You can check to see if adjectives are coordinate by seeing if you could place an **and** between them or if you could reverse their order without changing the meaning of the sentence.

The tired, chilled crowd began to leave the stadium.

Note that the sentence could have been written **The tired and chilled crowd began to leave the stadium,** or the adjectives **tired** and **chilled** could have been reversed without changing meaning.

The well-written, nicely designed report reached my desk today.

E. WITH NONRESTRICTIVE CLAUSES AND PHRASES

Separate nonrestrictive clauses and phrases from the other parts of the sentence by commas. A *nonrestrictive structure* is not essential to define or restrict the noun it modifies. A *restrictive structure* is essential to define or restrict the noun it modifies.

Examine these two sentences carefully:

The novel which was written by Fitzgerald remains my favorite.

The Great Gatsby, which was written by Fitzgerald, remains my favorite novel.

The clause **which was written by Fitzgerald** is needed in the first sentence to further limit the vague noun **novel.** Since the novel's title is given in the second sentence and there is only one novel with that title, the clause **which was written by Fitzgerald** is not necessary; it is separated from the other parts of the sentence by commas.

Sometimes the distinction between a restrictive and a nonrestrictive clause cannot be made without information in preceding or following sentences. In the following two-sentence sequence, it is clear which novel the writer is referring to in the second sentence; therefore, the clause is not necessary and should be set off with commas.

I reread *The Great Gatsby* for the fourth time last week. The novel, which was written by Fitzgerald, remains my favorite.

When you separate a nonrestrictive structure with commas, you are suggesting that the structure could be removed from the sentence without any serious loss. Be certain that is what you actually mean. Look at these examples:

All children who watch television excessively do poorly at school.

All children, who watch television excessively, do poorly at school.

The first sentence is what the writer intended. Those children **who watch television excessively** are the ones who do poorly at school. If you take out the clause in the second sentence — and that is what the commas suggest you can do — you get an untrue statement: **all children do poorly at school.**

Remember to use commas to set the clause or phrase off from other parts of the sentence only if its meaning is not essential to the sentence. *(See 2E for additional work with this problem.)*

Dr. Thadeus Constant, who teaches me Chemistry 312, has just published his first book.

The Wall Street Journal, which I read daily, presents much more than financial news.

He ate a gigantic sausage sandwich, piled high with pickles, while he watched television.

F. FOR DIRECT ADDRESS

Separate the name of a person you are directly addressing from the rest of the sentence with a comma.

Walter, please give me a hand with these boxes.

I understand, Dr. Leight, that you have an opening for a receptionist in your office.

Is my essay any better this time, Ms. Green?

G. FOR ELEMENTS OF CONTRAST

Use commas to separate parts of your sentence that mark a dramatic contrast to other sentence ideas.

She won the award for her poems, not her short stories.

It was Mark, not Eric, who called you last night.

You are in college to be educated, not to be entertained.

H. WITH TITLES, DATES, PLACES, AND ADDRESSES

Use a comma to separate a title or degree from an individual's proper name.

Faye Gossett, Accounts Manager

Nelson Gibson, M.D.

Use a comma to separate the day of the month from the year. When the month, date, and year are given in a sentence, separate the year from the rest of the sentence with a comma.

March 14, 1985

She remembers that it was August 17, 1978, when she first took her CPA examination.

Use commas to separate all individual items (street number and name, city, state) in an address. Do not use a comma between the name of the state and the zip code. When a city and state are given in a sentence, separate the state from the rest of the sentence with a comma.

1400 North State Parkway, Chicago, IL 60610

Houston, Texas

He arrived in Princeton, New Jersey, with twelve cents in his pocket.

I. WITH DIRECT QUOTATIONS

Use commas to separate direct quotations from other parts of

Professor Kilpatrick said, "If you pass this course, you are certain to do well in the next one too."

"If you pass this course," Professor Kilpatrick said, "you are certain to do well in the next one too."

"I want my mommy," the lost child wailed.

2. UNNECESSARY COMMAS

Inexperienced writers show a tendency to use too many commas, not too few. Here are some of the situations where unnecessary commas most often appear.

A. TO SEPARATE SUBJECT AND VERB

Never use a single comma to separate a subject from its verb.

INCORRECT

The members of my carpool, get along especially well.

The water pump on my car, is beginning to leak.

CORRECT

The members of my carpool get along especially well.

The water pump on my car is beginning to leak.

B. TO SEPARATE VERB AND OBJECT

Never use a single comma to separate a verb from its object.

INCORRECT

He reluctantly paid, the price.

My supervisor believes, that everyone can advance in the job.

CORRECT

He reluctantly paid the price.

My supervisor believes that everyone can advance in the job.

C. TO SEPARATE VERB AND COMPLEMENT

Never use a single comma to separate a verb from a complement.

INCORRECT

The flowers are, absolutely beautiful.

Marilee was, stunning in her prom dress.

CORRECT

The flowers are absolutely beautiful.

Marilee was stunning in her prom dress.

D. WITH COORDINATING CONJUNCTIONS

Never use a comma before a coordinating conjunction unless it joins two independent clauses or ends a series.

INCORRECT

I like everyone at work, but Bill.

Walking up the sidewalk, and appearing confident, Helen was really a bundle of nerves.

CORRECT

I like everyone at work but Bill.

Walking up the sidewalk and appearing confident, Helen was really a bundle of nerves.

Never use a comma after a coordinating conjunction.

INCORRECT

My brother works at the post office, but, he plans to quit.

The accounting text is expensive and, bulky.

CORRECT

My brother works at the post office, but he plans to quit.

The accounting text is expensive and bulky.

E. WITH RESTRICTIVE CLAUSES AND PHRASES

Remember that a restrictive structure *(see 1E)* is necessary for the intended meaning of the sentence. Do not separate it from other sentence parts by commas.

INCORRECT

The New Yorker, that you gave me last week, has a very funny story about living in the country.

The perfume, that she bought at Neiman-Marcus, was terribly expensive.

CORRECT

The New Yorker that you gave me last week has a very funny story about living in the country.

The perfume that she bought at Neiman-Marcus was terribly expensive.

3. THE SEMICOLON

A. TO SEPARATE INDEPENDENT CLAUSES

Use a semicolon to separate independent clauses not joined by coordinating conjunctions. The semicolon may be used alone or with a conjunctive adverb such as **however, therefore,** or **nevertheless.** When the semicolon is used with the conjunctive adverb, it is a common practice to follow the conjunctive adverb with a comma.

Martha Sue's goal is to become a lab technician; her parents insist that she become a doctor.

Martha Sue's goal is to become a lab technician; however, her parents insist that she become a doctor.

Wally just passed the examination for his pilot's license; therefore, he can take me flying with him now.

B. AS A SUPER COMMA

In some instances where you would ordinarily use a comma, you may need to use a semicolon as a kind of super comma, a stronger mark of punctuation than a comma. For instance, use a semicolon to separate items in a series if those items themselves already contain commas. Also, use a semicolon before a coordinating conjunction joining two independent clauses when there are already commas in those clauses.

Dr. Smith, Chairman of the Board; Ms. Lorenz, Director of Communications; and Professor Leibow, Financial Consultant; attended the meeting in Cleveland.

In the back of my closet, just behind all of the shoe boxes, I've hidden my diary; but even my mother, who knows everything, does not know this.

4. THE COLON

A. TO INTRODUCE A LIST, EXPLANATION, EXAMPLE, OR LONG QUOTATION

A colon, which indicates a significant break, is used to introduce a list, explanation, example, or long quotation. The material preceding a colon must be a complete sentence.

CORRECT

Bring the following items with you Monday: two pens, legal pad, note cards, and ruler.

Margaret Mead's statement about anxiety is still pertinent: "Worry in an empty contex means that men die daily little deaths. But good anxiety—not about things that were left undone long ago, but which return to haunt and harry men's minds, but active, vivid anxiety about what must be done and that quickly—binds men to life with an intense concern."

INCORRECT

The important ingredients are: sugar, nutmeg, and raisins.

The facts of the case: the location of the crime, the glasses left behind, and his familiarity with the worth of the jewels point to George as a prime suspect.

CORRECT

The important ingredients are these: sugar, nutmeg, and raisins.

The facts of the case which point to George as a prime suspect are these: the location of the crime, the glasses left behind, and his familiarity with the worth of the jewels.

The facts of the case—location of the crime, the glasses left behind, and his familiarity with the worth of the jewels—point to George as a prime suspect.

B. FOR REFERENCE TO TIME AND SCRIPTURE

Use a colon between the hour and minute when referring to time. Use a colon between the chapter and verse when referring to scripture.

3:30 P.M.   Luke 5:2

C. TO SEPARATE TITLES AND SUBTITLES

Use a colon to separate the title of a book from its subtitle.

Contact: A Textbook in Applied Communications

Robert Frost: An Assessment of His Worth

D. AFTER THE SALUTATION IN A BUSINESS LETTER

Use a colon after the salutation in a business letter.

Dear Mr. Prescott:

Dear Mr. Jordon:

5. THE PERIOD

A. AT THE END OF A SENTENCE

Use a period at the end of a sentence that makes a statement or gives a command.

The wind is supposed to stop late this afternoon.

Bring me the slacks that need mending.

B. IN ABBREVIATIONS

Use periods after most abbreviations.

Ms.　Mr.　Dr.　Ph.D.　M.D.　A.M.

Do not use periods in abbreviations that indicate company names or government agencies or that are pronounced as single words (acronyms).

ITT　IRS　CIA　FBI　NATO

If you are in doubt about how to punctuate an abbreviation, consult a good dictionary.

6. THE QUESTION MARK

Use a question mark after a direct question.

Why did you ever agree to a plan like that?

Which way did the car turn at this corner?

Do not use a question mark after an indirect question.

INCORRECT

Wanda wondered why no one had told her about the exhibit?

Mr. Ernst asked who had taken the file from his desk?

CORRECT

Wanda wondered why no one had told her about the exhibit.

Mr. Ernst asked who had taken the file from his desk.

7. THE EXCLAMATION MARK

The *exclamation mark* is used after an interjection, phrase, clause, or sentence to show surprise, disbelief, or any other dramatic emotion. Do not overuse the exclamation mark or it will become ineffective. Let your sentence structure and your word choice convey your feelings of emotion in most situations.

Ouch!

I frankly cannot believe what I am hearing!

"Holdup! Everyone on the floor!" the robber screamed.

8. THE DASH

Use a *dash* to set off material that represents a sudden break in thought from the remainder of the sentence.

The picnic—the one that had been planned for a full eight weeks—was cancelled at the last minute.

Mr. Grear said that the results were not ready because of a lack of clerical help to process them—a poor excuse if you ask me.

Use a dash to set off a parenthetical element and give it greater emphasis.

My brother-in-law—the one who is a judge—was arrested for drunken driving last weekend.

Unfortunately, I missed the final test in the course—the one that counted double.

9. PARENTHESES

Use *parentheses* to set off parenthetical material that you want to deemphasize.

A Modern Instance (written by William Dean Howells in 1882) is a perfect example of genteel realism.

When my mother was in the first grade (about 1937), she was the only girl in her class.

10. BRACKETS

Use *brackets* to insert editorial comments into material that is quoted directly.

"This novel *[August]* is clearly the hit of the summer."—Ben Rochester

"I frankly believe that it [the Vietnam War] marked a major turning point in American thought and action."—Edgar Slieve

11. ELLIPSIS MARKS

Use *ellipsis marks* (three periods with spaces before, after, and between them) to indicate that something has been omitted from a direct quotation. If the omission occurs at the end of a sentence, use three spaced periods for the ellipsis and insert the proper mark to end the sentence before the ellipsis marks.

My doctor said, "You must stop smoking immediately . . . if you want to live to be a grandfather."

"I frankly believe that it [the Vietnam War] marked a major turning point. . . ." —Edgar Slieve

PART III
MECHANICS

The punctuation marks discussed in Part II are necessary signals to guide your reader through what you have written. They are important to show the relationship of sentence parts; that is, they are an integral part of the sentence structure itself. Mechanics, on the other hand, are a part of what might more accurately be called the "print code." They do not function to make a sentence correct or incorrect. They are simply an agreed upon set of conventions for printing (or writing) certain kinds of information.

1. QUOTATION MARKS

A. FOR DIRECT QUOTATIONS

Use double quotation marks to mark the words of an exact quotation.

Ms. Heinrich said, "I know you hate to work evenings, but I really must ask you to come in tomorrow evening."

"The Germanic languages," Bruce Price wrote, "like to pile up nouns. The Romance languages virtually forbid it."

Long quotations — those four lines or longer — do not require quotation marks because they are presented in a special format that clearly identifies them as direct quotations. In a typed paper that is double spaced, for instance, the style required by the Modern Language Association calls for indenting the long quotation (sometimes called a ***block quotation***) ten spaces. This block format clearly separates the long quotation from the other text material.

In describing William Shenstone's fascination with the sights and sounds of the countryside, Samuel Johnson wrote:

> Now was excited his [Shenstone's] delight in rural pleasures, and his ambition of rural elegance: he began from time to time to point his prospects, to diversify his surface, to entangle his walks, and to wind his waters; which he did with such judgement and such fancy as made his little domain the envy of the great and the admiration of the skilful. . . .

One or two lines of a poem may be quoted within the sentence itself and identified by quotation marks. If you quote two lines of a poem, a slash mark (/) should be used to show where the first line ends.

Carl Sandburg affirms the power of the individual when he writes, "I am the people—the mob—the crowd—the mass."

Walt Whitman was describing innoence when he wrote, "The youngster and the red-faced girl turn aside up the bushy hill, / I peeringly view them from the top."

When you quote more than two lines of a poem, indent it as you would a long quotation in prose. Do not use quotation marks unless there is dialog in the poem itself.

Shelley begins his elegy "Adonais" with a general call to lamentation:

> I weep for Adonais—he is dead!
> O, weep for Adonais! though our tears
> Thaw not the frost which binds so dear a head!

B. FOR QUOTATIONS WITHIN QUOTATIONS

Use single quotation marks to indicate a direct quotation that is enclosed in another direct quotation.

Bryant commented, "Grandmother used to say 'be good to yourself in all the little ways' every time she left our home."

C. FOR TITLES OF CERTAIN WORKS

Use double quotation marks to indicate the titles of short stories, most poems, songs, and individual episodes of radio and television programs.

Our assignment for tomorrow is to read "A Clean, Well-Lighted Place."

I own fourteen recordings of "Memories."

Perhaps international politicians could profit from reading Robert Frost's poem "Mending Wall."

If the title is inside a direct quotation, it is marked with single quotation marks.

Our literature teacher said, "I expect everyone to read 'A Clean, Well-Lighted Place' carefully before tomorrow's class."

Long poems, generally those so long that they are published as complete books—Milton's *Paradise Lost,* for instance—are italicized just as are other book titles.

D. WITH END PUNCTUATION MARKS

The period and the comma should always be placed inside the quotation marks.

"Please listen carefully," Mr. Timmons said, "because I do not want to repeat the assignment."

The colon and the semicolon should always be placed outside the quotation marks.

The travel agent said, "It is imperative that you be at the airport an hour before your flight"; however, I thought I could cut that to forty-five minutes.

The question and the exclamation marks are placed inside the quotation marks when they are part of the quoted matter. They are placed outside the quotation marks when they relate to the entire statement.

My father asked, "Who moved my pipe tray?"

Have you read Adrienne Rich's poem "Not Somewhere Else, But Here"?

"You're fired!" he said emphatically.

2. ITALICS

Although printers have special type for italics, you should indicate italicized material in handwritten or typed copy by underlining it with a single line.

A. TITLES OF BOOKS, MAGAZINES, NEWSPAPERS, MOVIES, PLAYS, LONG POEMS, LONG MUSICAL WORKS, AND RADIO AND TELEVISION PROGRAMS

Last week's issue of *Time* is missing from my desk.

The Last of the Mohicans is one of Cooper's best novels.

I arrange my schedule so I never miss seeing *Another World.*

Have you seen the local opera's production of *Madama Butterfly?*

B. *FOREIGN* WORDS AND PHRASES, INCLUDING SCIENTIFIC TERMS

The judge ruled *ipso jure* that the automobile was certainly Gloria's and not Edward's.

The North American woodcock is a member of the *Philohela minor* family of game birds.

Certain foreign words have been used so frequently in English that they are considered a part of the English vocabulary and are not italicized. Among them are words such as **alumni, bassinet, catharsis, faux pas, hacienda,** and many others. If you are in doubt about whether or not to italicize a particular word or phrase, check a current dictionary.

C. NAMES OF SHIPS, PLANES, AND TRAINS

We had a delightful time touring the *Queen Mary.*

Air Force One is landing in Washington at the moment.

D. WORDS, LETTERS, OR FIGURES USED
    AS EXAMPLES OR ILLUSTRATIONS

Fran's excessive use of *pretty* and *marvelous* weakened the writing.

You know is one of the most overworked phrases that one hears.

The way you cross your *t's* may say something about your outlook on life.

3. HYPHENS

A. TO FORM A SINGLE ADJECTIVE

Use hyphens to join two or more words before a noun to form a single adjective.

the pea-green water   well-intentioned actions

ten-year-old child   forty-three-year-old woman

The hyphen is not used when the words come after the noun.

His actions were well intentioned.

The child was ten years old.

B. WITH COMPOUND NUMBERS AND FRACTIONS

Use a hyphen to write out compound numbers from twenty-one to ninety-nine.

twenty-five people   sixty-seven chairs

Use a hyphen for fractions that are compound modifiers.

a one-fourth mixture of water and oil

a one-third drop in sales

The hyphen is not generally used in other forms of fractions.

Sales dropped by at least one third last quarter.

Two thirds of the students passed the course quite easily.

C. TO JOIN PREFIXES AND SUFFIXES

The prefixes **all-**, **anti-**, **ex-**, **mid-**, **non-**, **self-**, and **great-** and the suffix **-elect** are frequently joined to their root words with a hyphen.

ex-marine   mid-October   self-motivated   secretary-elect

Many words are used so frequently with a specific prefix that the hyphen is dropped and the prefix and root word are considered as one. If you are in doubt about a specific word, check your dictionary.

antifreeze   midnight   nonentity

D. TO AVOID AMBIGUITY

Sometimes you need to use a hyphen to avoid either ambiguity or an awkward combination of words or letters. Compare these sentence pairs to see how important the hyphen is.

You need to resign your committee appointment.

You need to re-sign your committee report.

Yesterday I visited my favorite small-pet store.

Yesterday I visited my favorite small pet-store.

E. TO DIVIDE A WORD AT THE END OF A LINE

Use a hyphen to divide a word at the end of a written line. Remember that you can divide a word only between syllables.

auto-ma-tion   ambi-gu-ity   endo-cri-no-logy

Do not divide a word so that you have only one or two letters at the beginning or ending of a line. Do not, for instance, divide **a-bout, end-ed,** or **hard-ly.**

4. CAPITAL LETTERS

A. THE FIRST WORD OF A SENTENCE AND *I*

Always capitalize the first word of a sentence and always capitalize the pronoun **I.**

Why did you react in that manner?

She thought that I wanted the desk painted that color.

B. PROPER NAMES AND TITLES
PRECEDING PROPER NAMES

Capitalize all proper names of persons and places; geographic regions, names of streets, cities, and states; names of countries and languages; titles of organizations or institutions; names of religions or religious books; labels for political, racial, or social organizations, and words referring to the Deity.

Samuel Gotchamick lives in Miami, Florida.

Glynn learned to speak Urdu when he lived in West Pakistan.

The National Conference for Accountants will meet in New York this year.

My grandmother is an extremely devout Baptist.

The Supreme Being in the Moslem religion is called Allah.

Titles that precede a name are capitalized.

Governor Robert McHarry   Professor Jill Jennings

If the title follows the name, it is capitalized only in addresses and typed signatures of business letters. In the body of a piece of writing it is not capitalized.

TYPED SIGNATURE

Jill Jennings, Professor of English

IN TEXT

The report indicated that Jill Jennings, professor of English, said . . .

C. TITLES OF BOOKS, MOVIES, PLAYS, POEMS, PAMPHLETS, ETC.

Capitalize the first and last words of titles of works and all other words except articles, short prepositions, and short conjunctions.

The Red Badge of Courage

"On Reading"

"The Raven"

Word Processing for the Beginning Student

Articles, short prepositions, or conjunctions that are used as the first word of a subtitle are capitalized.

Writing Today: A Practical Rhetoric

"Visitation: Or Some Call It Love"

D. MONTHS, DAYS OF THE WEEK, AND HOLIDAYS

Capitalize the names of the months, days of the week and holidays.

Monday, February 10, 1985
Christmas   Rosh Hashanah

E. FIRST WORD OF A DIRECT QUOTATION

Capitalize the first word of a direct quotation.

"Everyone should arrive by mid-morning," she instructed.

Ms. Calmer asked, "Does everyone have the correct setting recorded now?"

If the quotation is interrupted, the second part is not capitalized unless the first part has an end-mark of punctuation.

"Everyone should arrive by mid-morning," she instructed, "and Kim will be responsible for providing supplies."

"Does everyone have the correct setting recorded now?" Ms. Calmer asked. "We can move on to the next step in the problem as soon as you are ready."

5. ABBREVIATIONS

A. WITH PROPER NAMES

Certain titles of address are customarily abbreviated when they come immediately before a proper name. These titles include the following: **Mr., Mrs., Ms., Dr.,** and **St.**

Mr. Whipple   Ms. Lawry   St. Thomas

Titles that show an individual's profession — **Prof., Capt., Rep., Sen.** — are abbreviated only when they are used with the full name. The title should be written out when it is used with the last name only.

Prof. George Wilson   Professor Wilson
Sen. Marianne Leads   Senator Leads

Certain other titles that customarily follow the name are also abbreviated. Among these are the following: **Jr., Sr., M.A., Ph.D, M.D.,** and others. Notice that these abbreviations are separated from the name by a comma.

Mr. George Wipple, Jr.   Ms. Lawry, M.A.

B. WITH INDICATIONS OF TIME

The standard indications of time are usually abbreviated.

5:15 P.M. (or p.m.)   6:30 A.M. (or a.m.)
12:10 CST (or C.S.T. or c.s.t.)
32 B.C.   A.D. 348

C. WITH NAMES OF DAYS, MONTHS, STREETS, CITIES, STATES, AND COUNTRIES

It is customary to abbreviate the names of days of the week, months of the year, streets, cities, states, and countries when they are part of the address of a letter.

5500 N. St. Louis Ave.	3214 Drane Ln.
Chicago, IL 60625	Dallas, TX 75241
Oct. 4, 1985	Dec. 7, 1986

These same items, however, should not be abbreviated when they are part of the text of an ordinary piece of writing.

He lives at 3214 Drane Lane, Dallas, Texas.
I want to see you Tuesday, November 17, in my office.

D. WITH RECOGNIZED NAMES OF COUNTRIES, ORGANIZATIONS, AND AGENCIES

The names of some countries, organizations, and agencies are almost always abbreviated. Here are some of the most common examples:

CBS	IBM	USA	USSR	
NAACP	NATO	UPI	GM	UCLA

Be certain that your reader will readily recognize and correctly interpret any abbreviation you use. It is generally wise to make sure that an abbreviation you are using appears in a good dictionary and is not just one that you have made up.

6. NUMBERS AND FIGURES

The guidelines for using numbers and figures vary somewhat according to the type of writing being produced. Nevertheless, you must be consistent. The following is a list of commonly used guidelines.

A. QUANTITIES ABOVE OR BELOW 100

Use figures for 100 and all quantities above 100; use words for all numbers below 100.

101 boxes of candy   345 votes   ninety-seven shirts

B. UNITS OF MEASUREMENT

Use figures for quantities below 100 when they are joined with a unit of measurement.

12 pints   48 ft.   75 days

C. SUMS OF MONEY

Use figures to express sums of money.

$15 (or 15 dollars) $0.35 (or 35 cents) $12.75

D. DECIMAL FRACTIONS

Use figures to express all decimal fractions.

7.023   18.55   0.45

E. FREQUENT REFERENCES

Use figures for any section of writing where references to them are frequent.

About 35 members of the 72 usually present met for some 65 minutes to take action on the 3 resolutions submitted.

F. ADJACENT FIGURES OR NUMBERS

When two numbers appear next to each other but represent a different unit of measurement, the shorter one is usually spelled out.

15 two-inch pans   two 25-member classes

G. ORDINARY FRACTIONS

Use words instead of figures to indicate ordinary fractions.

one-fourth   three and five-eighths

H. PERCENTAGES

Use figures to indicate percentages.

18 percent   75.5 percent

I. THE WORDS *MILLION* AND *BILLION*

Use the figures in front of the words **million** and **billion** when indicating quantity.

75 million dollars   1.5 million records

J. APPROXIMATIONS

Use words for numbers that are only approximate.

about sixty-five years ago

will cost around forty thousand dollars

K. LATITUDE, LONGITUDE, AND TEMPERATURE

Use figures to indicate latitude, longitude, and temperature.

45° South   99°F

L. INDICATIONS OF TIME

Use figures to indicate time when followed by either **A.M.** or **P.M.** but not when followed by **o'clock.**

4:14 P.M.   3:30 A.M.   five o'clock

7. SPELLING

Some people seem to be born spellers; others always have difficulty spelling words correctly. There is no quick cure for that latter group. If you know you are a poor speller, you must learn to use your dictionary as you proofread your writing. Don't trust your eye.

Actually, a large number of spelling errors can be classified according to type. Study the following sections carefully to see if you can determine the category (or categories) most of your spelling problems fit.

A. WORDS CONTAINING *IE*

In most English words, the letter **i** comes before the letter **e**.

chief   thief   field   belief   niece   achieve

There are two principal exceptions to this rule: (1) when the two letters follow a **c**, the **e** usually comes first and (2) when the **e** is pronounced as a long **a** (as in neighbor and weigh), it comes before the **i**.

ceiling   conceit   deceit   receipt

neighbor   weigh   sleigh   vein   heir

Exceptions to the ie guidelines are these: either, neither, leisure, height, weird, seize, fiery, and species.

B. FINAL *E* AND *Y* WORDS

Words ending with a final **e** sometimes change spelling when a suffix is added.

If the suffix begins with a vowel, delete the final **e**.

changing   coming   hoping   excitable

If the suffix begins with a consonant, keep the final **e**.

hopeful   hopeless   lovely   advertisement   sincerely

Exceptions to these guidelines are these: argument, courageous, dyeing, noticeable, ninth, and truly.

Words ending with a final **y** also sometimes change spelling when a suffix is added.

If the letter before the **y** is a consonant, the **y** changes to an **i.**

flier   tries   reliance   fiftieth

If the suffix being added begins with an **i,** do not change the **y.**

flying   crying   dying   replying.

If the letter before the **y** is a vowel, do not change the **y.**

played   saying   praying   stayed

C. DOUBLED LETTERS

Some words double their final letter before adding a suffix. This usually happens when the word is one syllable long and ends in a consonant with a single vowel coming before it.

running   clapping   planning   planned

Do not double the final letter in a one syllable word if it ends with two consonants or if two vowels precede the final consonant.

rasping   gasping   gasped   fielding   peeled

Double the final consonant of a word with more than one syllable if it ends with a consonant preceded by a single vowel and if it is accented on the final syllable.

preferred   preferring   conferred   (all accented on the last syllable)

D. PLURALS

Most nouns are made plural simply by the addition of an **s**.

apple**s**   kid**s**   desk**s**   toy**s**   bird**s**   street**s**

Some words that end in **f** or **fe** change the ending to **ve** before adding the final **s**.

life/li**ves**   elf/el**ves**   thief/thie**ves**   wife/wi**ves**

Nouns ending in **s, ch, sh,** or **x** are made plural by adding **es**.

dish**es**   wish**es**   tax**es**   church**es**

If a noun ends with a **y** preceded by a consonant, make the noun plural by changing the **y** to **i** and adding **es**.

cit**ies**   countr**ies**   suppl**ies**   traged**ies**

If a vowel precedes the final **y**, simply add an **s**.

day**s**   valley**s**   turkey**s**   donkey**s**

Nouns that end with an **o** preceded by a consonant usually add **es** to form their plural.

potato**es**   tomato**es**   zero**es**

Exceptions to this guideline include the following words:

jumbo**s**, hypo**s**, auto**s**, piano**s**, soprano**s**, and pro**s**.

Some words change forms completely to show plurality.

man/men   child/children   mouse/mice   goose/geese

Some words retain a plural form from their original language, usually Latin.

alumna/alumnae   curriculum/curricula   criterion/criteria

Combined words form their plural by adding an **s** to the base word.

brother**s**-in-law   editor**s**-in-chief

A letter, number, or abbreviation forms its plural by adding an apostrophe and an **s.**

A**'s**   C**'s**   5**'s**   Ibid.**'s**

E. CONFUSED PAIRS

Words such as **compliment** and **complement** sound exactly the same but have entirely different meanings. Other words such as **accept** and **except** sound very nearly alike but also have entirely different meanings. Be certain to use the correct spelling for the meaning that you intend. Check the word in your dictionary if necessary.

Here is a list of some of the most frequently confused word sets.

accept, except	board, bored
advice, advise	born, borne
affect, effect	canvas, canvass
alley, ally	capital, capitol
already, all ready	censor, censure
altar, alter	choose, chose
altogether, all together	cite, sight, site
always, all ways	clothes, cloths
assistance, assistants	coarse, course
bare, bear	complement, compliment
birth, berth	conscience, conscious

council, counsel
descent, decent, dissent
desert, dessert
dominant, dominate
fair, fare
farther, further
formerly, formally
forth, fourth
hear, here
heard, herd
hole, whole
its, it's
later, latter
lesson, lessen
lightning, lightening
lesson, lessen
maybe, may be
minor, miner
moral, morale
passed, past
patience, patients
peace, piece

personal, personnel
plain, plane
precede, proceed
presence, presents
principle, principal
prophecy, prophesy
quiet, quite, quit
respectfully, respectively
right, rite, write
sense, since
stationary, stationery
statue, stature, statute
straight, strait
than, then
their, there, they're
through, thorough, throw
to, too, two
tract, track
weather, whether
who's, whose
your, you're

F. PRONUNCIATION AND SPELLING

Some words are frequently misspelled because they are also
frequently mispronounced. Look at the following list of some
words that often fall into this category:

INCORRECT	CORRECT
asterik	asterisk
canidate	candidate
excape	escape
everthing	everything
Febuary	February
goverment	government
hunderd	hundred

INCORRECT	CORRECT
liberry	library
preform	perform
perscribe	prescribe
quanity	quantity
reconize	recognize
strickly	strictly
tradgedy, trategy	tragedy
nucular	nuclear

Sometimes errors in pronunciation are really errors in syllabication. If you put an extra syllable into a word when you say it or if you take one out, the chances are rather good that you will do the same thing when you write that word. Look at these examples:

INCORRECT	CORRECT
athelete	athlete
barbrous	barbarous
boundry	boundary
disasterous	disastrous
genrally	generally
grievious	grievous
literture	literature
sophmore	sophomore
temperture	temperature
temperment	temperament

If you find yourself misspelling the same word again and again, always misspelling it in the same way, chances are quite good that you mispronounce the word. Check the correct pronunciation in your dictionary.

PART IV
WRITING
PARAGRAPHS
AND ESSAYS

1. GETTING STARTED

A. FINDING A SUBJECT

Perhaps the most common complaint of a student writer is that he or she cannot think of anything to write about. In fact, students often spend hours pondering various ideas for a composition, in the end writing on a topic that does not particularly interest them. If they are not interested in their topic, their readers won't be either. Good writing comes from an ideal mix of writer and topic. It happens when the writer selects a topic in which he or she is deeply interested and conveys that interest to a reader.

As a student writer, you are often simply assigned a topic and told to write about it. When this happens, you must work within given confines. Very often, though, such topics are broad — urban living in the 1980s, for instance — you have the opportunity to focus or narrow that topic. In this way you can virtually carve your own specific topic out of the general one by limiting the broad topic to a much narrower one in which you are interested. A sociology major, for instance, might write on the plight of the urban elderly in the 1980s. An economics major might focus on the limitations of tax revenues for urban improvements during the 1980s. (For additional ideas on limiting the topic, *see 2.*)

You should also begin building a reserve of ideas to write about for those occasions when you have flexibility in selecting the topic. Actually, you already have that reserve. The steps listed in this section merely formalize the process for you.

Free Write

Make a point of sitting in some quiet place at rather frequent intervals and doing free writing. In free writing you simply agree with yourself to write for a designated period of time. You do not stop to think in depth about any one idea; you keep your mind working and your ideas flowing. You do not worry about spelling, punctuation, or grammar. The purpose of free writing is to make your subconscious thoughts conscious and get them on paper. Just relax your mind and write. Free writing does not need to be organized or logical. You might begin by writing about what you did last Saturday night, suddenly find yourself criticizing the movie you saw on television, and then flash back to why you had not washed the car that afternoon.

Free writing helps you to focus on ideas or sets of ideas you may hardly be aware of having. The more you free write, the more you will begin to detect certain patterns in your ideas. And as you reflect on some of your free writing ideas, you will begin to see possible topics for your compositions. You might, for instance, decide to write a paper explaining why the movie was bad. Or you might explain to your father why you failed to wash the car Saturday afternoon. Free writing helps you to find and isolate some of the ideas that churn through your mind daily.

Interest List

Begin to make a list of your major interests. As a start, you might put broad areas of interest in a notebook—one broad area at the top of each page. Under each broad area, list the questions that you imagine someone else might ask you about this topic. Those questions can eventually be refocused, if necessary, and turned into thesis sentences or specific ideas to lend direction to your writing. Look at the following example:

Tropical Fish

How long have you kept tropical fish?
What kinds of fish do you like best?
How many different tanks do you have?
How expensive is it to raise tropical fish?
If I wanted to raise tropical fish, how should I get started?

These questions came from a student's interest list. The student had many more interests, each listed on a separate page, but he put a wealth of focused information on this short page alone. From the broad topic—tropical fish—and the five questions, the student might develop any number of thesis statements or sentences that would lend a specific direction to his or her writing. Here are just a few of the possibilities:

I got my first pair of guppies when I was seven and have kept tropical fish ever since.

Although I have kept tropical fish for only eight months now, I become more involved with them every day.

My favorite tropical fish are the multicolored guppies with their large, graceful tails.

While it is difficult to pick a favorite from among my twenty-two fish, I think I probably like the two albino cats the best.

I started with one 10-gallon tank, and now I have sixteen tanks of various sizes scattered throughout the house.

I presently have a tank for my live breeders, a tank for my babies, a hospital tank, and a special display tank for my two black angels.

By working together with several other friends who have tropical fish, I keep my weekly expenses down to just under six dollars.

Getting all of my tanks set up and stocked cost me well over three hundred dollars, but now I spend only about six dollars a week for supplies.

The beginner is well advised to start with a 10-gallon tank and to begin with only two or three types of live breeders.

The beginner must be extremely cautious to buy fish from a reputable supplier and to avoid any store that has either cloudy tanks or sick fish.

Brainstorm

You may find that your best ideas often come not in isolation but as products of an exchange of ideas with other individuals. Such exchange sessions can be quite informal or quite formal. You can learn to take advantage of them all. Become an active participant in informal conversations in the cafeteria, in the hallway, on the bus. What are people talking about? What dominant ideas continue to surface almost daily? You should interject your own ideas into these informal discussion groups. Ask questions. Try to get people to defend various positions. When you have left the group, think about what occurred. What new information did you learn about the topic? about human behavior? How might you use some of this information for a writing assignment?

Although you can certainly gather some valid ideas from informal discussion groups, they are not actual brainstorming sessions. A real brainstorming session takes place when a group of people gets together to discuss one designated topic: for example, how student activity fees should be divided among various campus groups or why the campus news-paper is nothing more than a gossip rag. There is no formal structure to the session, no official leader, no motions, no rules. Everyone simply presents his or her ideas to the entire group. The various ideas put forward usually generate debates. Some ideas are accepted, expanded, and improved. Others are rejected. A brainstorming session, actually a problem-solving technique borrowed from business and industry, simply pools a large number of minds and lets them explore a single issue.

The next time your class has a broad writing-topic assigned, you might invite several of your classmates to join you for a brainstorming session on the topic. Whether the broad topic is bird imagery in Keats or covert FBI activities during World War II, you will be surprised to discover how helpful it is to hear others talk about the topic. As the session continues, you will find your own ideas taking form as your mind is stimulated by the collective thinking of the group.

Journal Writing

You will probably find it helpful to keep a daily journal in which you write about the broad topics that will eventually be presented in your compositions. Journal writing is more focused than the free writing activities described earlier in this section. In journal writing, you begin with a broad subject and begin to write about it in an effort to find something of special interest to you.

Suppose your assignment is an essay, due in two weeks, on attitudes toward the elderly. You should commit yourself to writing a page or so in your journal each day for several days. These exploratory pages permit you to try out ideas, to move from one limited topic to another, to test your own level of interest. More than likely, a pattern will emerge. You may find that on Tuesday you want to continue the same phase of the topic you began on Monday — a good clue that you found that phase interesting. You may also find yourself repeating variations of a central idea from one day to the next.

Here are some excerpts from a student's journal. On each of the indicated days, she filled a page or more on some phase of the topic. Later she used a highlighter to underscore the common ideas that seemed to run throughout the journal:

Monday

> When I was a young girl, my favorite month was July because that was when we always went to see my grandfather. We called him Pop. I don't know how old I was before I realized that he had another first name: Clarence.

Wednesday

> For the life of me I just can't understand how some people can treat old folks with such disrespect. Last week when I went to Sheila's to study biology with her, I saw her grandmother in

the kitchen. No one spoke to her; no one tried to introduce me to her. Everyone pretended that she wasn't there. The poor old woman could hardly walk, but she was in the kitchen trying to make herself a sandwich. Obviously no one had invited her to the table for dinner.

Thursday

Last summer I went with my parents to New York. It was the first time that I had ever been to a large city, and I was excited and frightened at the same time. Even now I can recollect images of the old women, they called them bag ladies, walking the streets, carrying everything they owned in two or three tattered sacks. No one paid them any attention as they sifted through garbage sacks in search of part of a sandwich or maybe a Coke can with a few sips left. That was who bothered me the most: everyone just pretended that they did not exist.

Saturday

I was thirteen when Mother explained to me that Grandpa could no longer live by himself and would have to move in with us. Although I still loved him, I admit some serious thoughts when I learned that he would move into my room and I would have

101

to sleep on a day bed in the den. Why did he have to live with us? Why didn't he go live with Uncle Alex? Why couldn't he sleep on the day bed? Then he came. I had not seen him in nearly a year, and he had changed. He was stooped almost double and he could hear only if I shouted right in his ear. I cried and cried that night, partly because I was angry and partly because I was afraid. The next morning he called me to help him walk to the kitchen, as he would call me every morning for nine years. Slowly I grew to love that morning ritual. We walked slowly and shouted at each other about the weather, my school work, the quality of the morning's coffee. I learned a lot from Pop about life and about people. Those were the fastest nine years I can possibly imagine.

This student wrote much more material in her journal, but she found the information about old people helpful. She collected some common ideas which could be bound together into an essay on a topic about which she obviously felt quite keenly. From the information in the journal, she formed the following thesis sentence:

I know from my own experience the value of caring for an older person and the injustice of ignoring them.

Another advantage of using the journal technique is that it frequently provides you with some sentences, clauses, and phrases that you can work directly into your essay. Although they may need some polishing, the ideas are there. You may often find that you can pull large chunks of material out of your journal and use them effectively as rough draft copy for your essay.

B. LIMITING THE SUBJECT

Some of the material in the section above relates as much to limiting your subject as it does to finding it. In reality, most writers perform the two tasks at the same time. It might be worthwhile, however, to discuss some practical concerns specifically related to limiting your subject.

Required Length

Consider the length of your final composition. You can write far more in twenty-five pages than you can in five. The amount of space dictates the types of information and the quantity of detail you can include. If your instructor has asked for a 500-to-700-word essay, you cannot adequately discuss the effects of the Great Depression on American society. Your writing would be too general and would deal with only the obvious. You might, however, develop an interesting paper in which you examined the effect of the Great Depression on your grandfather or some other member of your family. Remember that writing becomes interesting when it provides details. Do not plan only broad, sweeping comments with little room left for detail.

Deadline

Consider the amount of time you have to work on the project. You sometimes have more time to work on certain projects than you do on others. Before you commit yourself to a final topic, you should think about the work you would need to do to develop it. Will you have to do some library research? Will you have to read for background information? Will you have to gather ideas by talking with other people? Finally, do you have the time to do all these things? For instance, if you are going to write an essay on the effects of the Great Depression on your grandfather, you will need to talk with him or gather information from your parents or other relatives. Can you get all this done in time to write your paper? If not, you must restrict the range of your topic even more.

Purpose

Consider the purpose of your writing. You should remember that writing aims to accomplish a purpose and limit your topic to work toward that purpose. The three most commonly recognized purposes for writing are to entertain, to inform, and persuade. An essay on how the Great Depression affected your grandfather would inform. Thus it would not be a good topic if your instructor had asked that you write a composition to entertain.

If you were given the broad topic of **vacations,** you might limit it according to your purpose and come up with something like the following:

TO ENTERTAIN

I had such a silly, fun time when I went with my two cousins to Mexico.

TO INFORM

If you are planning to travel by air on your next vacation, you should know how to get the lowest possible fares.

TO PERSUADE

No matter how busy you think you are or how strapped you might be for money, you owe it to yourself to take an annual vacation.

Journalistic Questions

Consider the journalistic questions as limiting devices. Reporters focus their writing by asking **who, what, when, where, why,** and **how.** By asking these questions about your broad topic, you will often discover a limited and interesting focus. Suppose your broad topic is **cooking.** Here are some possible journalistic questions:

WHO

Who does the cooking in your family? Who is the best cook that you have ever known?

WHAT

What kind of cooking do you like the best? What attitude does your mother (father, aunt, cousin) have toward cooking?

WHEN

When were you first taught how to cook? When does the cook in your family prepare a special meal?

WHERE

Where did your mother (father, aunt, cousin) learn to cook? When you were a small child, where did you sit to watch your mother cook?

Why do you enjoy cooking so much? Why do you think your aunt is such a good cook and your mother is not?

How does the cook in your family plan a typical meal? How are cooking secrets passed from generation to generation in your family?

Any of the single questions listed above is more limited than the general topic of **cooking.** If you ask several of these questions during the planning stages, you might be able to combine two or more of your answers into a limited topic about which you are truly interested. Putting together the answers to some of the questions listed above, for instance, you might decide that you enjoy cooking because you learned it from the best cook in your family, your Aunt Millie, who taught you to cook when you were only seven years old.

2. SEEING ORGANIZATIONAL PATTERNS

A. LOOKING AT THE DETAILS

As you limit your topic and as ideas related to your topic appear in your journal or in your conversations with friends, you should begin to realize that you have a large quantity of unorganized information. At this stage of the writing process, you are exactly where you should be. You should not get started on a writing task with a preconceived idea about organization; rather, you should let the organization develop from the types of information you ultimately have to work with and from the intended purpose of your writing.

At some point, you need to jot down the specific ideas you might want to use in your paper. At this stage, there is no need to worry about complete sentences or proper sequences. Simply make a list of ideas as they occur to you or as you pull them out of your free writing or journal. A list of ideas for the writing topic discussed above might look something like this:

seven years old

lived in Springfield

aunt Millie moved there from Denver

my favorite aunt

had six kids of her own

not much money

everyone in family had to help

big kitchen, everyone ate together

cooking was kind of act of love

family visited in kitchen while she worked

marvelous chocolate pies and tiny pecan cookies

laughed and sang while she cooked

worked in old jeans most of time

sat me on chair beside her

got to stir the batter

finally made my first cake — awful

got better with her help

   had baked first one far too long

asked me to help her cook for party

made it all seem fun

mother amused

liked to do things for other people

brought me a cookbook for eighth birthday

   still have it

These details were jotted down as the writer thought about them. Some are more complete than others; some already have subdivisions. At this stage, the important thing is to get your ideas down without worrying about the final paper. First you need to see what you have to work with; then you can decide about organization, additional information, and style.

B. ORGANIZING THE DETAILS

Although there are various methods for developing your ideas *(see types of development discussed in 4D)*, there are really only three ways to organize your material: order of importance, order of time, and order of space.

Order of Importance

Probably the ordering system most frequently used is that of importance. As you look at the list of ideas, you regroup those ideas into the order of their importance, remembering that the sequence in which ideas pop into your mind may not be the sequence you want to use for writing about them.

You may arrange ideas according to their importance by moving either from the most important to the least important or from the least important to the most important. To a large extent, the pattern you select depends on your topic and on your purpose.

If your objective is to provide your reader with information, you will probably present the material in a pattern that moves from most important to the least important. Readers sometimes do not read a report thoroughly from beginning to end. They read the first few paragraphs carefully and then skim hurriedly the rest of the report. By putting your most important ideas at the beginning, you increase the chance that your readers will see them and give them appropriate attention.

If your goal is to get your reader to take a specific action — such as sending in a contribution, signing a petition, or appearing at a committee meeting — you are probably better off moving from the least important to the most important.

Thus you save your best, most dramatic reason so that it comes just before your final appeal for action.

Suppose you are upset because the circulation time for your institution's library is two weeks, not nearly enough time for you to read assigned books and take notes. You decide to talk with the dean to determine why the present policy exists. Then you decide to write a brief report for the campus newspaper, detailing the administration's justification for the present system.

Because you are writing only to provide information, you will probably arrange that information according to the order of decreasing importance. If so, your thesis sentence and the information that you gathered would look like this:

Dean Wilson contends that there are five strong arguments in favor of the present two-week circulation policy at our library.

1. Too many students and too few books to allow a longer time.
2. System keeps fines to a minimum.
3. Long periods result in more lost books.
4. This system is used at most area colleges.
5. This system has been in successful operation here for over fifteen years.

Suppose you want to write a different kind of essay, one in which your purpose is to persuade the administration of your college to extend the circulation period. Because you would probably want to end your essay with a direct appeal for action, you would save your strongest arguments so that they come just before your appeal. Therefore, you would arrange your ideas in an order from least important to most important. Your information and the final appeal might be arranged something like this:

1. Twin Basins College, in the next town, just extended its circulation period to three weeks.
2. Student survey supports longer time.
3. Library staff cannot document "lost book" theory.
4. Short system simply makes library look good by churning books constantly.
5. Administrative concern with tightening academic demands requires that students be given more time for serious research.

In light of the arguments contained in this report, I am asking the Administrative Advisory Council to recommend an extension of the circulation period to three weeks.

Order of Time

Certain types of topics almost demand chronological organization. If you are giving instructions to someone, you arrange your ideas in time sequence. **First, you do this . . . then you do this . . . afterwards you do this.** If you are attempting to show that a certain situation — racial prejudice, for instance — has existed for many years, you are likely to develop your ideas in a chronological sequence: **During Colonial America . . . before the Civil War . . . after the Civil War . . . during this century.**

In some writing situations, you might want to work with a reverse time sequence, moving backward instead of forward. For instance, if you are attempting to analyze the roots of racial prejudice in this country, you might find it more effective to write about racial prejudice during this century and then to work backward, ending with the racial attitudes of Colonial America.

Narrative writing also normally orders information by time. If you are recalling an experience or telling a story, you probably describe events in the order in which they took place. Although you might begin with a present setting to grab your reader's attention and then flash back, your organizational pattern is still chronological. If you were arranging the material about Aunt Millie's cooking *(see 2B)*, you would certainly use a time pattern.

Order of Space

Your last organizational option is that of space. This type of pattern, used mainly in descriptive writing, arranges items in relation to other objects around them, as they exist in relation to the space they occupy. Good descriptive writing usually moves in a decided pattern. The most common patterns are these:

top-to-bottom / bottom-to-top
left-to-right / right-to-left
near-to-far / far-to-near
large-to-small / small-to-large
clockwise / counterclockwise

The system you decide to use should depend upon the objects you are describing and your purpose. If you are writing about the Sears Tower in Chicago or the World Trade Center in New York and your purpose is to focus on the height of the building, you will probably use a top-to-bottom or bottom-to-top system. If you wanted to describe the interior of a large cathedral and its impact on you when you first entered, you would probably use the far-to-near or the near-to-far system. In deciding which pattern to use, you will find it helpful to think of yourself—your point of view as the writer—as a movie camera photographing the same scene. Would the camera move up and down? left to right? Would it zoom to the far and then back to the near? You should not randomly jump around from one focal point to another but develop your detail much as a movie camera would record it, moving slowly from one scene to another in a prearranged system.

3. WRITING THE PARAGRAPH

A paragraph is a set of sentences related to the same topic. Seen by many writers as a miniature essay, the paragraph is, indeed, organized and developed with the same rhetorical techniques used in a full-length essay. It most often has a **topic sentence** (similar to the **thesis sentence** of an essay) which serves as a point of unification for all of the other sentences. The details within a paragraph are organized according to one of the three patterns discussed in the previous section: order of importance, order of time, or order of space.

Using paragraphs effectively is another way to help your reader understand your writing more clearly. Your paragraphing shows something about how you grouped thoughts in your own mind. When your reader sees a new paragraph, marked by appropriate indentation, he or she knows that you are moving to another phase of the topic or that you are shifting to a different type of support. When you use transition words or phrases as you move from one paragraph to another, the reader can also understand the relationship that you see between the ideas in one paragraph and those in another.

A. TOPIC SENTENCES

The **topic sentence** announces the topic of your paragraph and limits that topic. By carefully wording a topic sentence,

113

you, the writer, can focus and shape your thinking. The carefully worded topic sentence also helps your reader by focusing for him or her the ideas you are going to write about and by showing the limitations you are placing on yourself as the writer.

The most common place for the topic sentence is at the head of the paragraph. You have probably heard at some point the three time-honored rules of writing: tell your reader what you are going to do, do it, and then tell your reader what you have done. This basic formula for the introduction, body, and conclusion works even within a unit as small as the paragraph. Putting the topic sentence first tells your reader exactly what you are going to do.

Although the beginning of the paragraph is the best place for you as a novice writer to put your topic sentence, you will eventually learn to use it effectively elsewhere in the paragraph. Experienced writers often have it follow one or more transitional sentences that begin the paragraph. In paragraphs that build to a climax, they often place the topic sentence last, where it serves as a kind of summary or comment upon what they have written. Experienced writers do not necessarily include a topic sentence in **every** paragraph; they sometimes prefer merely to imply their main idea.

As a beginning writer, however, you would be wise to put a topic sentence at the beginning of each paragraph, for a topic sentence in this position gives you and your reader a clear direction.

A good topic sentence must be specific. If it is too vague or too broad, you have not focused your ideas, you have not given your reader any assistance. The topic sentence should also limit your topic. In a single paragraph, you cannot write adequately about Robert Frost's attitudes toward nature, but you might examine the image of snow in one specific poem:

TOO BROAD

Robert Frost's use of snow in his poems creates negative feelings.

RESTRICTED

In "Stopping by Woods on a Snowy Evening," Robert Frost uses snow images to suggest death.

You should include words or phrases in your topic sentence to tell your reader what to look for in the paragraph. If you say there are **three reasons** why something exists, the reader will look for those three reasons. If you use a word like **type, kind,** or **class,** your reader looks for divisions into types, kinds, or classes. Similarly, if you mention **similarities** or **contrasts,** your reader anticipates development by comparison or contrast.

Here are three extremely broad topic sentences followed by rewrites of each. Notice how each has been rewritten to give it more focus and to provide some clues of how the paragraph will be developed.

TOO BROAD

I enjoy doing office work.

Mr. Roberts is a better teacher than Mr. Lawrence.

The dates I have had these past few months were certainly strange.

RESTRICTED

My three favorite assignments in the office are answering the phone, processing cash receipts, and working on the computer.

Mr. Roberts is a better teacher than Mr. Lawrence because he explains concepts more slowly and uses clever, memorable illustrations to make his points.

The dates I have had these past few months have all been space cadets, zombies, or television freaks.

B. SUPPORTING DETAILS

You should always remember that writing becomes interesting at the level of its detail. Your topic sentence announces the subject to be developed in the paragraph, but it does not develop the subject. Your supporting details do.

As a writer, you must decide how many details to include. Usually, that decision is based on what you know about your reader and your purpose. If you are writing a memo to someone you work with announcing an office picnic, you need few details. If you are writing directions for operating a particular piece of office machinery to someone not at all familiar with it, you need a great many details.

One of the most effective ways to think about the details that should be included in a paragraph is to think of them as structured layers of support. Suppose you are going to write a paragraph about three of the most effective teachers you have ever had. Your paragraph structure might look something like this:

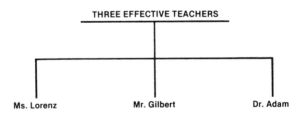

THREE EFFECTIVE TEACHERS

Ms. Lorenz   **Mr. Gilbert**   **Dr. Adam**

Using this scheme, you might write a paragraph with only major levels of support. In this pattern, each sentence in the paragraph directly supports and modifies the topic sentence. Your paragraph would read something like this:

During my fourteen years of schooling, I think that I have had only three truly effective teachers. Ms. Lorenz, my fifth grade teacher, did more to excite me about learning than anyone I can remember. Then in the eleventh grade Mr. Gilbert convinced me that the library was a wonderful place. Finally, my present biology teacher, Dr. Adam, has made me look forward to class in a way that I never thought possible.

Although there are no grammatical errors in the paragraph above, and although each sentence supports the topic sentence, the writer does not offer sufficient details to develop the thesis. The reader wonders how Ms. Lorenz excited the writer, how Mr. Gilbert made the library such an interesting place, or why Dr. Adam's class was so interesting that the writer looks forward to it.

To develop a paragraph, you should certainly think first of major support sentences. After all, you have to decide what major ideas you want to include. After that, however, you need to provide supporting details. When you do this, you are adding minor support sentences to your major supports. Your structure would look something like this:

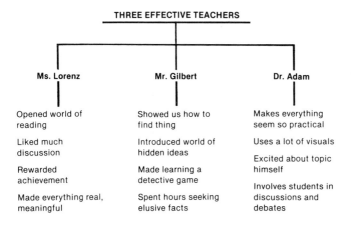

THREE EFFECTIVE TEACHERS

Ms. Lorenz	**Mr. Gilbert**	**Dr. Adam**
Opened world of reading	Showed us how to find thing	Makes everything seem so practical
Liked much discussion	Introduced world of hidden ideas	Uses a lot of visuals
Rewarded achievement	Made learning a detective game	Excited about topic himself
Made everything real, meaningful	Spent hours seeking elusive facts	Involves students in discussions and debates

Once you added these details to your paragraph, it might look something like this:

During my fourteen years of schooling, I think that I have had only three truly effective teachers. Ms. Lorenz, my fifth grade teacher, did more to excite me about learning than anyone I can remember. She introduced me to the larger world of reading with all its excitement and to the world of lively discussion and debate which so often follows good reading. She rewarded my accomplishments by a bit of praise, followed immediately by another challenging assignment; but in the process she made everything seem real and meaningful. Then in the eleventh grade Mr. Gilbert convinced me that the library was a wonderful place. He spent hours in the library showing us how to use the resources there to find needed information, how to search quickly for that one special hidden idea. He made library research seem like a kind of detective game in which we were all willing to spend hours and hours trying to find elusive facts that we knew were there somewhere. Finally, my present biology teacher, Dr. Adam, has made me look forward to class in a way that I never thought possible. He has an uncanny ability to make everything seem so practical as he presents ideas with his carefully developed set of pictures, posters, and graphics. As Dr. Adam conducts the class, his own enthusiasm is contagious. Anyone so excited about his subject just has to excite others. And the heated discussions and debates prove just how excited his students can become.

You could add even more layers of detail to what you have here. For instance, you might want to write about some particular books that Ms. Lorenz introduced to you or describe one or more of the challenging assignments that she gave. You might want to explain how Mr. Gilbert taught you to use the library effectively or to discuss one of the detective-type games he assigned. If you added that third level of detail to this paragraph — detail to modify your details — you would probably break the paragraph into three separate paragraphs: one for each of your teachers.

As you add supporting details to your paragraph, remember that you have only three ways to organize those details *(see 2B)*. The sample paragraph above, for instance, makes effective use of **time order.**

C. UNITY

As mentioned earlier *(see 3A),* the topic sentence announces what you are going to write about and serves as a kind of anchor around which all of your ideas cluster. Once you have presented the topic of your paragraph, every sentence in that paragraph must support your topic sentence. *Paragraph unity* means just that: every sentence supports the topic sentence. If one or more of your sentences do not support the topic sentence, you have violated paragraph unity; and your reader is likely to be confused to find sentences that are not clearly related to what you say you are writing about.

The necessity to maintain unity within the paragraph is another reason why you must word the topic sentence carefully. If you write your topic sentence carefully and are aware of its range and its limitations, you are less likely to add sentences that do not fall within your announced scope.

If you are writing about the tasks you like to do in the office, you would probably violate unity to write about how you dress for your office job. This material would fit only if you were explaining that you have to dress a special way to perform a specific task. In the sentences within your paragraphs for unity, be especially aware of the restrictions that you yourself have imposed by placing limiting words or phrases in the topic sentence:

My kitten has the **cutest little face.**
Entire paragraph must be developed to show the kitten's cute face. To look at any other aspects of the kitten in this paragraph would violate unity.

The movie you recommended to me was a real **bore.**
You can give only evidence why you found the movie boring. You cannot write about the lighting or seating in the theater or about the stale popcorn you also had.

Examine the following paragraph carefully. You should understand clearly why the sentences in boldface violate paragraph unity and should be removed.

As her wedding date approached, I think that I was almost as excited as my sister. She claims she did not sleep at all the week before the wedding, and I don't really think I did either. **Usually I go to bed about 10:30 and sleep until around 7:30.** I know that at least two of those nights we sat up all night reviewing plans, checking to see that we had done everything on our "to do" list. Two days before the wedding, my excitement had reached such a peak that I didn't even eat. Maybe I had borrowed love from my sister and was living on it, but I just went sailing through the day, full of energy and not the least bit hungry. **My brother Tim came in from college that afternoon. He is a senior medical student and always takes everything very calmly.** On the day of the wedding, I was up at 4:30 in the morning, shouting at everyone to get up, this was the day. I even began to get dressed for the wedding an hour before my sister did. And after I was dressed in my bridesmaid's gown, I couldn't sit down. I just paced the floor—for an entire hour. On the way to the church, I first got the giggles and then the hiccups. I don't think I could take having a sister get married very often.

D. TRANSITIONS

One of the characteristics of a good paragraph is its *coherence;* its various parts should be joined together, not strung together. By learning to use transitions effectively you are learning one of the most important ways of achieving coherence within a paragraph. Always remember your responsibility as writer to do whatever is necessary to help the reader follow your thought processes. Transition words and phrases tell your reader exactly how you see the relationship between two ideas.

Not all transition words and phrases do the same thing. Some are used when you want to add an idea, others when you want to contrast an idea, and still others when you want to provide an example or illustration. Here are some of the most commonly used transition words or phrases:

also	furthermore	on the contrary
although	however	on the other hand
but	in fact	similarly
especially	in general	still
finally	likewise	though
first	moreover	whereas
for example	nevertheless	yet
for instance	notwithstanding	
for one thing	occasionally	

Another way to provide transition and thus reinforce the coherence of your paragraph is to repeat key words or phrases or to use synonyms that refer to them. If your topic sentence says that a movie is bad because of its **poor dialog** and **weak acting,** you should pick up these words and use them at appropriate points in the paragraph. When you are giving evidence of the poor dialog, use words like **dialog, speech, talk, language.** When you move to the part of the paragraph that comments upon the weak acting, use words and phrases like **act, inept acting, perform, boring performance**. This effective use of the repetition of key words or ideas reinforces the relationship you see among the various ideas in your paragraph and helps to hold the paragraph parts together.

Although there may be various points within a paragraph that require transition to make your intended meaning clearer, it is especially important that you use transition devices between the major support sections. In the sample paragraph on three effective teachers presented earlier, the word **Then** introduces the second major level of support, and **Finally** introduces the third. Become accustomed to providing this type of necessary link as you move from one idea to another.

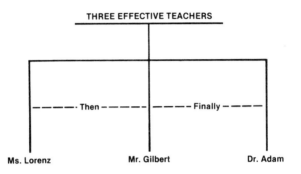

THREE EFFECTIVE TEACHERS

— — — — · Then — — — — · — — — — Finally — — — — —

Ms. Lorenz   **Mr. Gilbert**   **Dr. Adam**

4. WRITING THE ESSAY

Because an essay is composed of a group of paragraphs arranged in a manner that develops a central idea, virtually everything said about paragraphs in the previous section applies to the essay as well. An essay must have a central purpose, in this case stated in the thesis sentence. Just like the paragraph, the essay must have sufficient detail, all related to the thesis sentence, to develop its topic and to make it interesting. And the essay, like the paragraph, must make use of effective transition devices to move the reader along from one thought to another.

A. THESIS SENTENCE

In an essay, the ***thesis sentence*** functions in the same way the topic sentence functions in a paragraph. It announces your thesis: the central idea you intend to develop. Because the thesis is your own—something you intend to demonstrate—a reader should be able to understand your position or attitude toward the subject by reading the thesis sentence alone. A good thesis sentence usually indicates to the reader the method that you are going to use to develop your topic.

Here are some weak thesis sentences:

I am going to write an essay to explain why I feel the student activities fee should be lowered.

You need not call attention to the fact that you are writing an essay; and unless you are writing an essay that requires first person development, you should keep the pronoun **I** out of your thesis.

Going to the movies is a lot of fun.

Is the topic of this essay "going to the movies" or "fun"? Both are too broad to function adequately. The sentence gives no specifics of the writer's point of view, no indication of how the ideas will be developed. It is a top-of-the-head sentence that will probably lead to nothing more than top-of-the-head writing. In addition, be-verbs are weak; in a thesis sentence, they weaken what should be the most forceful sentence in the essay.

There are three reasons why I had to quit my job.

There is an extremely weak word for starting a sentence as important as the thesis sentence, and this weak word is followed by an equally weak be-verb. This sentence is also weak because it is so formulaic. It could be made to fit hundreds of topics just by changing its ending. There are three reasons why (fill in almost anything).

You can learn a lot about people by just sitting and watching them.

You should be certain the **you** in a thesis sentence is really justified. Are you writing to a specific **you?** Would **one, a person,** or **an individual** be better? This sentence is also vague because it gives no specifics about the topic and offers no indication of how the writer intends to develop it.

The ideas suggested by the weak thesis sentences above could be refocused and rephrased to make them much more effective:

The student activities fee should be lowered because the present fee is an undue burden on many students and the student board does not need the additional money.

The sentence now permits the subject of the paper to serve as the subject of the sentence; further, it suggests the divisions the writer will use in developing the topic.

If one selects wisely, attending the movies offers the potential for an inexpensive evening of entertainment.

The sentence is now focused so that the writer can give emphasis to the importance of selecting movies wisely if one wishes to be adequately and inexpensively entertained.

I finally had to quit my job at the paint factory because it interfered with my studies, left me no time for a social life, and frequently depressed me.

The writer has now included reasons in the thesis sentence. The sentence is no longer formulaic; it could not be used with a multitude of possible topics.

By just sitting and watching other people, an individual can quickly determine who is pleased with life and who is discontented.

The sentence indicates the ideas the writer will explore, the specific characteristic an individual can learn about others just by watching them.

B. PARTITIO STATEMENT

A common problem among the weak thesis sentences above was that they gave no indication of direction for the essay's development. Remember that the more help you give your reader the better. One of the best helps that you can provide is the *partitio statement.*

The partitio statement indicates the nature of the parts you will examine to develop your topic, that is, the divisions of your topic. By including a partitio statement along with your thesis statement, you provide your reader with a road map of your essay. You say, in effect, I am going to write about this; then I am going to move on to write about that; and finally I am going to write about yet another aspect of my topic. Seeing the signs, an alert reader begins to look for those topic divisions.

As demonstrated in the examples above, a partitio statement can often be included in the thesis sentence:

The student activities fee should be lowered because the present fee is an undue burden on many students and the student board does not need the additional money.

The essay is clearly going to be divided into two parts. In the first half the writer will examine the hardship that the present fee causes many students; in the second, he or she will prove that the additional money is not really needed.

I finally had to quit my job in the paint factory because it interfered with my studies, left me no time for a social life, and frequently depressed me.

This essay will contain three parts in its development. Because the partitio statement is intended to guide the reader, you should develop the ideas in your essay in the order they are announced in your partitio statement.

If the thesis sentence itself is extremely complex or if a listing of the parts might become extremely lengthy, the partitio statement may come immediately after the thesis sentence:

Several poems reflecting a melancholy fascination with death at least partially countermand Robert Browning's image as a dashing lover and man about town. Among the major poems dominated by his melancholia are "Rabbi Ben Ezra," "Prospice," and "Epilogue to Asolando."

Because of the complexity of the thesis sentence, this partitio statement functions more effectively as a separate sentence.

After eighteen weeks of frustration, the workers' collective outrage finally began to produce results. Management agreed to investigate the possibility of a more comprehensive medical coverage, to set aside and equip one entire floor of the plant as an exercise gym, and to rent an adjacent building and convert it into a day care center.

The infinitive clauses in the partitio statement are necessarily lengthy. In instances like this, the thesis sentence would be weakened if the partitio statement were part of it. Both work more effectively as separate sentences.

C. THE INTRODUCTION

The introduction to your essay should capture your readers' attention. It serves the same purpose as a display window in a large department store. That window is designed to stop shoppers as they pass by, get their attention, and attract them inside. The introduction to an essay should function in the same manner. It should arrest the readers' attention and make them want to "come inside," that is, read the body of the essay to see what is there.

Some kinds of writing can begin directly with the thesis sentence, but most writing is more effective if it begins with an attention-getting device. If you are writing a business analysis for your supervisor at work, you may be able to begin your report directly, assuming that your supervisor will read what you have written because it relates to a common interest — your jobs. If you are answering an essay question in an examination, your teacher is probably more interested in how well you have synthesized the facts of the course than in how well you can capture his or her attention.

In most instances, however, you should use an attention-getting device. When you do, the thesis sentence and the partitio statement come immediately afterwards. The two may be placed at the end of the attention-getting paragraph or, if that paragraph is long or complicated, in the next paragraph.

Here are some proven methods for developing attention-getting devices. You should, of course, consider both your subject and your audience before you decide which one to use.

Narrative Introduction

You might begin with a short narrative. Relate something you have experienced or heard about that will lead you directly into the subject. For instance, if you are presenting the plight of the elderly in America, you might develop an introduction like this:

I first met Anna about a year ago. Actually, we didn't meet then; I just saw her behind my neighborhood grocery store digging through the garbage cans hunting for something to eat. About a month later, with winter rapidly approaching, I saw her there again. This time I tried to engage her in conversation, but she was wary of a stranger with two full bags of groceries and wandered up the street. At a discreet distance I followed her until I saw her step into a tiny alley and slip unobtrusively into a large refrigerator packing crate—her home. The next day I left some bread and cheese outside her unique house; when I drove by thirty minutes later, it was gone. The following day I left a thermos of homemade soup. The next day the empty thermos was sitting outside her door. On the third day I took her a large basket of fruit and rapped gently. Slowly she opened the crate's door and took the fruit, silently. Nearly two weeks later she trusted me enough to talk. For nearly four months now I have been visiting with Anna almost every day. During this time I have heard horror stories of the abuse of our elderly that make me furious. Even in our small community we must do what we can for our elderly to correct injustices in medical care, to provide safe housing, and to incorporate them into the fabric of our society.

This introduction tells a story (narrative) about Anna and her impact on the writer's life. The paragraph ends with a thesis sentence that also contains a partitio statement. Notice that the specifics of the partitio statement are not spelled out in the Anna narrative; rather they are saved for development in the body of the essay.

Sometimes humor may effectively be used as a part of the narrative beginning. Unfortunately, humor is much more an oral art than a written one. A story that is funny when it is told with facial expressions, vocal inflections, and heightened use of gestures often dies on paper. To be effective, humor must both be related to your subject matter and be fresh. A stale joke will not suffice.

Statistical Introduction

You might also begin with a set of statistics. For some topics, an impressive set of statistics will lend strength to your ideas if they are startling enough to arrest attention.

According to a recent study published by Dr. Houghton, 78 percent of our elderly receive totally inadequate medical care; 52 percent live in housing that, for one reason or another, is substandard or unsafe; and 89 percent feel that they are no longer a part of society and begin to withdraw from the world they so desperately need. Even in our small community we must do what we can to change these percentages, to see that our elderly do receive proper medical care, do have adequate and safe housing, and do feel that they belong to our society. After all, we need them as much as they need us.

This introduction uses statistics both to highlight the subject and to introduce the divisions of the essay. To reinforce the partitio, the writer restates it in the conclusion of the introduction.

Shocking Introduction

If you begin with a startling or controversial statement, you can sometimes get the attention of your audience by shocking them. A bold or even controversial statement at the beginning of your introduction does the job.

Instead of trying to lengthen life, we should try to shorten it. With all that is going on around us, we simply do not have time or resources to care for the unproductive members of our society.

Although no one would say it, our collective society makes this statement every day in the manner in which it neglects the medical, housing, and social needs of our elderly. Even in our small community we must take steps to correct these injustices.

This introduction makes a shocking statement, but the writer then uses the controversial statement as a springboard for getting at the real subject: neglect and abuse of the elderly.

Quotation Introduction

A carefully chosen quotation is sometimes an effective way to begin your introduction. Be certain that the quotation fits your topic and that you do not have to force it to work. For a quotation to be truly effective, it is also important that your audience be familiar with your source and that your source be someone of recognized authority. An extremely powerful quotation from Andrew Schwartz would have very little effect if the audience had never heard of Andrew Schwartz. Similarly, a quotation from your cousin, uncle, or best friend is not nearly as effective as is one from a person recognized as an authority in the area being presented.

James Joyce captured the pitiful feeling of many elderly persons when he wrote, "I am passing out. O bitter ending! I'll slip away before they're up. They'll never see. Nor know. Nor miss me. And it's old and old it's sad and old it's sad." But old and sad should not—must not—be thought of as the same. We must change all of that. We must take whatever steps are necessary to provide our elderly with the personal and physical comforts that will put a lie to Joyce's dramatic description.

This introduction uses a quotation from James Joyce that is at the same time dramatic and melancholy. Both the language and the tone of the quotation lend themselves to the swift movement to the thesis of the essay as it is described in this introduction.

Rhetorical Questions

Rhetorical questions can be effective openers because they are addressed directly to your audience and thus demand audience participation. Research has also shown that a series of questions in parallel patterns is far more effective than a single question.

What would you do if you knew that your own mother might eventually be denied medical care just because hospitals have no room for any more old folk? What would you do if you knew that she would have to spend the last years of her life in a run-down building with no fire alarms and little heat? What would you do if you knew that some clubs, churches, and even some of her "younger" friends would not want her around because the presence of old people creates a negative image?

If you knew these things about your own mother's future, you would probably first become angry and then try to correct these social evils. While it may not be your own mother, somebody's mother is experiencing these injustices right now. Even in our small community we must work harder to meet the medical and housing needs of our elderly and to see to it that they are welcomed members of all of our social groups.

The parallel beginnings of the first three sentences in this introduction work to pull the reader inside. Once the reader has begun to move into the essay, pulled almost subconsciously by the rhythm of the three opening sentences, the writer can make a shift to the thesis of the essay.

D. THE BODY

The way you develop the body of your essay will vary considerably, depending upon your topic and your purpose. Although there are several different ways of arranging ideas in an essay, one of the most useful methods is to apply techniques from the *modes of discourse.*

These modes—illustration, classification, comparison/ contrast, definition, and analysis—are not strangers to you. Rather, they are classifications of the ways you think every day. Not a day goes by that you do not illustrate something in your mind or compare and contrast two or more objects (even if they are nothing more than two different hamburgers or two different milkshakes). By reviewing these modes of discourse, you will be able to understand how they work as units of thought. You will then be able to apply some of these principles in developing the body of your essays.

Illustration

Illustration, sometimes called *exemplification,* is the developmental technique you use most often. Throughout the day you are illustrating, or giving examples, to make statements convincing. You burst into the cafeteria for your morning coffee and announce to a friend, "That game last night was the worst I have ever seen." Then you set about illustrating just how bad the game was by telling what happened. You illustrate with such statements as "Let me show you" or "Let me give you an example."

Developing an idea by illustration requires that you give specific proof to support whatever general idea is suggested by the thesis sentence. If you begin, for instance, by "That game last night was the worst I have ever seen," then you must offer one or more examples to support your control word: **worst.** Good advice to remember is that you should **show, not tell,** when writing illustration. Remember that the purpose of illustration is to make specific by way of example. If your thesis sentence says your new neighbors are an asset to the community, don't merely **say** that they are already doing a lot of good. Instead, give one or more examples of the good things they are doing; show them doing good in one or more narrative sequences.

Most of the time when you need to illustrate an idea, you will find yourself using narrative — telling a story or series of stories to make your meaning more precise. Whether you use one narrative incident or several depends upon your topic and, in some instances, the way you phrase it in your thesis sentence. If that sentence is **Yesterday was absolutely the most horrible day that I have ever experienced,** you might develop it in one of two ways: write in some detail about the single crisis which made yesterday so bad or write about the several crises, starting at 9 in the morning and ending at 7 in the evening, which made yesterday so horrible. If, on the other hand, your thesis sentence reads **The experiences I had at work today will affect me for years to come,** you are obliged to develop a series of narratives.

Remember, that narratives, at least in the shortened format you use to illustrate, are arranged chronologically. And since you will usually be writing about something that has happened in the past, be very careful with your verb tenses. Do not shift unnecessarily from one tense to another.

Classification

Classification is another type of development you use quite frequently. Throughout the day, you classify your friends, your teachers, kinds of music, and types of cars. Classifying things permits you to provide them with some order, at least in your mind. You probably already have the clothes in your closet arranged according to some scheme of classification: dress clothes, school clothes, work clothes, and play clothes, for instance. When you use a notebook with labels such as **Biology, Math, English, History** or **Information Science,** you are already classifying your academic subjects.

Classification takes a varied set of items and groups them in classes or categories. Libraries classify books according to such labels as **Fiction, History,** or **Biography.** Without thinking too seriously about it, you have already classified your friends into categories: **best friends, average friends,** and **casual friends.**

A good way to see how classification works is to see it broken into a schematic.

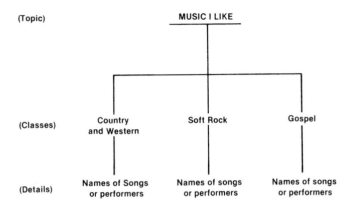

(Topic)   MUSIC I LIKE

(Classes)   Country   Soft Rock   Gospel
             and Western

(Details)   Names of Songs   Names of songs   Names of songs
             or performers   or performers   or performers

Notice that this topic is limited. The writer is not going to classify **all** music, just the music that he or she likes.

An essay developed according to classification often uses a word like **kinds, types, classes,** or **categories** in the thesis sentence. This word tells the reader to look for separate divisions or categories of the broad general subject. A shorter essay would probably have a paragraph for each of the classes. A longer essay would probably have several paragraphs on each of the classes.

If your topic sentence reads **Although I like different kinds of music, I spend most of my time listening to gospel,** the organizational pattern, based on the schematic above, becomes clear. You would develop a paragraph or more about your admiration for country and western music, naming some favorite songs or performers along the way; then you would do exactly the same thing with soft rock music. Finally, you would offer even more specifics about your favorite: gospel. That final section of the essay might well be introduced by a transition sentence something like this: **Although I do spend a lot of time listening to country** and western and soft rock, **I spend twice that much time listening to gospel.** You would then develop sufficient details to justify gospel music's favored status.

Comparison and Contrast

You constantly *compare* and *contrast* things: your English teacher with your friend's English teacher, hamburgers at McDonald's with hamburgers at Burger King, a Ford with a Chevrolet, or this year's baseball team with last year's. Although for some topics you may be comparing (looking at similarities) more than contrasting (looking at differences) and with others the process may be reversed, in reality it is almost impossible to do one without doing some of the other.

As with all other types of writing, comparison and contrast is used for a specific reason. The purpose of comparison and contrast writing is usually to make a judgment, to say that your English teacher is better than your friend's English teacher, or that hamburgers at one place are better than hamburgers at another.

Because you are making a judgment, you must be fair in your examination of the objects you are studying. You should, for instance, examine the same aspects of both objects. If you were to compare a Ford with a Chevrolet to determine which one to buy, it would be unfair to write about the purchase price of the Ford without mentioning the purchase price of the Chevrolet.

After you have carefully thought about your topic and found the aspects you wish to compare and contrast (finding those aspects is actually a form of classification), your next step is to arrange the material. You have two general choices: the *whole-by-whole* method or the *part-by-part* method. In the former, you write everything you intend to say about one object and then everything you want to say about the other. In the latter, you examine the two objects simultaneously, looking at an aspect of one and then the same aspect of the other and then another aspect of the first and the same aspect of the other. Although there is no hard and fast rule, most writers agree that the whole-by-whole method is more effective with short pieces of writing and the part-by-part technique is more effective with long pieces of writing. Here is a working outline showing how the same topic might be set up according to each of the different methods:

WHOLE-BY-WHOLE METHOD

Facts about my teacher	Facts about Kim's teacher
strict discipline	virtually no discipline
clearly defined objectives	no apparent objectives
lot of homework	almost no homework
rigorous tests	easy take-home tests
fair grading standards	grades on personalities

PART-BY-PART METHOD

Type of discipline	Difficulty of tests
my teacher	my teacher
Kim's teacher	Kim's teacher
Educational objectives	Grading policy
my teacher	my teacher
Kim's teacher	Kim's teacher
Quantity of homework	
my teacher	
Kim's teacher	

Like an essay developed by classification, one developed by comparison and contrast often uses words in the thesis sentence that indicate to the reader the type of development being used. You may elect to use words like **similarities,** differences, comparisons, or contrasts in your thesis sentence; or you may prefer simply to imply a comparison or contrast. Frequently you will be able to structure the thesis sentence so that it contains a partitio statement which lists the specific aspects of the items being examined. Here are some sample thesis sentences:

Although I have eaten at George's Steak House several times, its price, service, and ambience do not compare well with those at Maxwell's Steaks.

The rhythm, tone, and images used by Shelley in "To a Skylark" make his a far more positive poem than Keats's "Ode to a Nightingale."

Having gone to both a parochial and a public high school, I can honestly say that their similarities far outweigh their differences.

Definition

Defining terms or concepts is an extremely important part of the process of communicating. Many arguments result from nothing more than two parties defining terms differently. Skilled debaters learn the importance of defining the key words in their resolution in order to aid their cause.

Without being completely aware of it, you probably use definitions every day. Most of these take the form of a synonym or a simple explanation. These one-sentence definitions look something like this:

To **alleviate** one's burden means to make it more bearable, to reduce it.

A **gamp** is a very large, baggy umbrella.

A **pastille** is a small, medicated or flavored tablet.

A **kinescope** is the television tube that changes electical signals into pictures.

137

Actually, one-sentence definitions fit the formula for a formal definition. That formula requires that you place the word you are defining into a class or family (a gamp is a kind of umbrella, a pastille is a kind of tablet). Then you show how the term differs from other members of that class or family (gamps are large and baggy; the pastille is small and is always medicated or flavored). The formal structure looks like this:

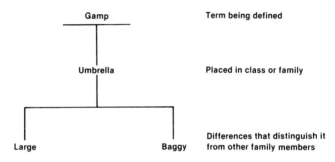

Often you will need to write sentence or paragraph definitions as a part of your essay. Sometimes you may want to write an entire essay that is an extended definition. Such an essay can be developed in any of the following ways:

- Tracing the changing meaning of the word from one time period to another.
- Offering illustrations that will define the word by example.
- Showing how the word might be understood differently by different audiences.
- Examining the differences between the denotative and connotative meanings of the word.

Analysis

Another method of development is *analysis*. Analysis is similar to classification in that it breaks its topic into component parts, but it is different in that it seeks to analyze the relationship among those component parts. Actually, there are two types of analysis: *causal analysis* and *process analysis.*

Causal analysis begins with a recognized fact—you woke up this morning with a bad cold, you made the best grade in the entire class on your calculus test, your city council just raised taxes by 15 percent—and then seeks to determine what has caused this fact to be true.

When you develop an essay by causal analysis, begin with the recognized fact and then analyze the probable causes which have contributed to that fact. For some topics you might arrange your causes in chronological order; for others you might prefer to use order of importance.

You should be careful to include a discussion of all probable causes. A single cause seldom produces a result. Most results are the product of several different causes. Think about it as a mathematical equation:

cause 1 + cause 2 + cause 3 + cause 4 = result

As you develop your essay, you will probably devote one or more paragraphs to each of the causes you present. The organization of a typical causal analysis essay looks something like this:

Statement of Result	Our city council has just announced an increase of 15 percent in city taxes.
Cause #1	• City budget is $1.2 million in the red
Cause #2	• Must negotiate new salary scale with fire and police personnel this year
Cause #3	• Major streets need repaving
Cause #4	• Not an election year so no negative political effects at this time

4D **IV WRITING PARAGRAPHS AND ESSAYS**

Process analysis deals with the processes or steps one must go through to accomplish a certain end product. When you give directions, you use process analysis. You are telling someone the processes involved in getting, for example, to the nearest post office. When you give instructions on how to do a particular task or explain how a specific machine or instrument works, you use process analysis.

A major requirement for essays developed by process analysis is that they be ordered chronologically. The reader must be able to see the sequence that he or she is to follow to build a model railroad, bake a quiche, or repair a fuel pump. If you are giving instructions to your reader, develop your essay in the second person:

If **you** will follow these easy steps . . .

Next, **you** should blend . . .

Finally, add three cups of . . . (implied subject)

If you are writing to a reader who will convey your message to another party, write in the third person:

If **he** wants to improve his grade, **Bill** needs to . . .

Next week **he** should submit . . .

Be certain to include all the steps necessary for someone to perform the task you are describing. You should not take for granted, for instance, that the reader knows that the flour in the recipe should be sifted. Include this information as one of the steps in your sequence. Also, be certain to define or illustrate any terms or concepts that your reader may not readily undestand. It is scarcely helpful to tell someone to check a car's butterfly valve unless you also tell that person where the butterfly valve is and what it looks like (manuals of instruction often include pictures).

140

The process essay usually begins with a thesis sentence that states what task is being undertaken. Because the paper itself is usually arranged in steps necessary to perform a task, the thesis sentence often indicates how many steps are in the process:

By following these five easy steps, you can grow tomatoes inside your own home.

Removing the old wax from your kitchen floor is not difficult if you follow these four steps.

If you have the time, wallpapering your own room is an inexpensive and enjoyable way to change its entire image.

The organization of the essay follows the various steps that are necessary. In a full-length essay explaining how to do something, you would probably devote one or more paragraphs to each of your steps. Because these individual steps are so important to the process, be certain to use transition markers **(next, when that is completed, following that, the third thing to do, finally)** to help your reader move along from one step in the process to another.

E. THE CONCLUSION

Some writers have difficulty ending an essay effectively; they just can't seem to let go. A good conclusion is as important as a good introduction. You do not want the last impression to be sour.

An effective conclusion should be brief and forceful. You have undoubtedly heard speakers who announced they were about to end their talks but then continued for another twenty minutes. Remember them when you begin your conclusion. Bring it to an end! Although long essays may require conclusions of several paragraphs, most short essays — the kind you typically write in college classes — can be concluded in a brief paragraph, sometimes in one strongly worded sentence.

Your conclusion should "sound and feel" like a conclusion. That is, your reader should know when he or she begins to read it that you are wrapping up your essay. You can accomplish this goal by using key transition words at the beginning of your concluding paragraph or, in some instances, by referring to the entire body of the essay:

Finally, it becomes clear to the observer that . . .

In essence, then, the choices are few . . .

From this evidence, one can see . . .

The arguments just presented require a response . . .

The conclusion should summarize the main idea(s) of your essay. Sometimes it need be nothing more than a careful rewording of your thesis sentence. Sometimes, especially in longer essays, it may include a rewording of the thesis sentence and the partitio statement. If you have presented different theories in the body of your essay, your conclusion might briefly summarize them and point the reader to a simple, single summary statement. If you began your essay with a narrative, you might link your conclusion to some aspect of that narrative, but you shouldn't tell the story over again. Do not let a quotation alone serve as your conclusion. No single quotation could possibly summarize exactly what **you** have written. You might use a quotation as a part of your conclusion, typically at the very end, after you have summarized your major points.

Here are two different conclusions, each effective in its own way:

The evidence presented here is shocking, and that is exactly its intended purpose. It may take shocks like this to outrage the citizens of our community into taking specific action against the injustices our elderly suffer all too silently. If so, we should be shocked more often.

I know that I will never forget Anna and I hope that you will never forget some of the startling evidence presented here, evidence which proves that there are hundreds of Annas living in our midst. In the presence of such overwhelming evidence, we have no choice but to begin to correct the injustices about which we are now so vividly aware. Adequate medical care, comfortable housing, and social acceptance are what our elderly need. We must give them nothing less.

5. REVISING

Good writing is often the product of good revising. Not even the most experienced writers "get it right" the first time. You should learn to think of the act of composing as having four parts:

1. **Gathering and Limiting Ideas.** In this prewriting part, you let your mind wander through the possibilities surrounding your topic with the sole purpose of seeing exactly what material you have. The sections "Finding a Subject" *(1A)* and "Limiting the Subject" *(1B)* both deal with aspects of the work to be done before you begin to write.

2. **Writing the Rough Draft.** This is the first conversion of your ideas into sentences and paragraphs, the first effort to make them "say" something. Remember that writing is itself a process of discovery. As you write about a specific topic, you discover what you think about it. Thus your rough draft does not reflect the final ideas about your topic that you will reach;

rather it documents your mind's work on the topic. The rough draft permits you to get some of your ideas on paper so you can evaluate them more carefully.

3. **Editing the Rough Draft.** When you begin to edit, you look at your rough draft (and any subsequent drafts before your final paper) and make changes in organization and development, style, or usage and mechanics. Suggestions for things to look for as you edit are given in "A Revision Checklist" *(5A).*

4. **Preparing Final Copy.** The final copy is the version you submit to your instructor or, perhaps, to your supervisor. This copy should conform to whatever specific format standards you have been given. It should be clean and neat and it should look finished. It should not look like another draft, full of crossouts or whiteouts.

The revision checklist which follows indicates some of the more important things you should look for as you edit the drafts of your essay. Some experienced writers can read a paper through once and look for virtually all the things mentioned in this checklist; other writers find that they must read a paper through two or three times, editing for different types of problems each time. Remember that the editing process may require you to write several drafts. You may rewrite an essay once to change your organization or to provide more development for some especially weak parts; then you may rewrite it again to make stylistic changes that further improve the finished product.

A. A REVISION CHECKLIST

Organization and Development

- Does the essay develop the topic announced in the thesis? If the essay is written for a specific assignment, does it meet the requirements of that assignment?
- Is the thesis sentence precise? Does it suggest anything about the organization of the essay?
- Is there an obvious system of organization throughout the essay?
- Are enough details provided for the various parts of the essay?
- Is the space devoted to the various parts proportionate to their importance to the topic as a whole?
- Are appropriate transitions provided from one major part of the essay to another?
- Does the paragraphing function properly to develop the ideas of the larger essay without breaking those ideas into small, meaningless units?
- Is the conclusion satisfactory? Does it "let go" of the essay cleanly?

Style

- Is the diction of the essay appropriate to the subject?
- Is there evidence of a variety of sentence lengths?
- Is there a variety among sentence patterns?
- Are verbs carefully chosen?
- Except where necessary, has the passive voice been avoided?

- Have clichés been avoided?
- Are any words used so often that they become boring or jarring?
- Is the diction specific rather than general?

Usage and Mechanics

- Is every group of words punctuated as a sentence actually a complete sentence?
- Have run-on sentences been avoided?
- Do subjects and verbs agree?
- Is the correct verb tense used in every instance?
- Has consistency of tense been maintained throughout the essay?
- Do pronouns reflect the correct case and number?
- Has consistency of person been maintained throughout the essay?
- Do all sentences begin with a capital letter and end with appropriate end punctuation?
- Are all internal marks of punctuation correct?
- Are all words correctly spelled?

6. THE DEVELOPMENT OF AN ESSAY

On the following pages you will be able to follow the development of a short paper from its prewriting stage through the rough draft and editing processes to the finished product. First, here is the prewriting list that the student prepared as he planned to write his paper on a memorable event.

visiting Grandpa at the hospital

- about 6 yrs old
- remember driving in Grandma's old Buick
- hot inside (legs sticking to seats)
- Mom was upset; knew he was dying
- remember being in lobby, couldn't go upstairs
- security yelled at me for being noisy
- old man, tall and skinny, with baggy pants
- very busy, a lot of noise and bustle
- people in white smocks walking by
- security still watching me
- becoming very fidgety and bored
- lots of people, some in wheel chairs
- Grandma and Mother come back downstairs
  and tell me about Grandpa

— said he was doing ok.
— died two weeks later

Next, by working from his prewriting list and arranging materials into chronological order, the student wrote the following rough draft:

My visit to the hospital to see my sick Grandfather is an experience I will always remember.
I was six, riding in a hot, stuffy car, with my
legs sticking to the vinyl seats. My mom was
upset because she knew he was dying of cancer.
Walking to the hospital desk, we found out that
children under ten couldn't see patients. I was
supposed to see him, I thought. Very confused,
I sat in the lobby. I remember being in the lobby
and a skinny old security guard told me to behave.
He had pants that bagged on him as he walked back
and forth in the lobby. The hospital must have
had a busy day, because all I could see were
people in white smocks darting around. I felt
very uneasy with the noise and the mean security
guard watching me constantly. Tied down to the
couch, I became very bored. An hour had passed

and my mother and grandmother, both with sullen
faces, walked to the desk. I got up, ignoring the
guard, walked to the desk and talked to Mom. They
explained that Grandpa was doing well. I could
see them hide their emotions not to upset me. He
died two weeks later.

Working through suggestions found in the Revision
Checklist, the student edited his rough draft as follows:

"sick" isn't necessary

movement of "I...
remember" to the
beginning sharpens
the focus.

My visit to the hospital to

see my ~~sick~~ Grandfather is ~~an~~

~~experience~~ (I will always

— more detail

remember.) I was ~~six~~, riding

in a hot, stuffy car, with my

legs sticking to the vinyl-covered

seats. My mom was upset

– violates perspective

– "walking" adds
nothing

(because she knew he was dying

                        at
of cancer.) ~~Walking~~ to the

hospital desk, we found out

— more details here

that children under ten ~~couldn't~~

— more details about his feelings

~~were not permitted in patients' rooms.~~
see patients. I was supposed

I was upset!

"waited" is stronger

to see him, I thought. ~~Very~~

Why couldn't I? *waited*

/ ~~Confused~~, I ~~sat~~/ in the lobby, /

wordiness is eliminated

where

I remember being in the lobby

again choppy — combine

~~and~~ a skinny old security guard

watched my every move. His

~~told me to behave. He had~~

— "shuffled" is stronger, so is "across"

pants that bagged ~~on him~~ as

shuffled   *across*

he ~~walked~~ back and forth ~~in~~

room

the ~~lobby~~. The hospital ~~must~~

~~have had a~~ busy day, because

wordiness is eliminated

~~all I could~~ see were people

were

in white smocks, darting around.

"scared" is stronger

was scared by

I ~~felt very uneasy with~~ the

noise and the mean security

guard watching me constantly.

Confined
~~Tied~~ down to the couch, I

About
became very bored. An hour

later
~~had passed and~~ my mother and

— "tied down" is too colloquial

grandmother, both with sullen

Came out of my grandfather's room and
faces, walked to the desk.

~~I got up;~~ Ignoring the guard, *I*

more details to effect the chronological order

walked to the desk and talked

Crying she
to Mom. ~~They~~ explained that

"she" explains

but
Grandpa was doing well, I *still*

not   him.
could see ~~them hide their~~

~~emotions not to upset me.~~ He

— violates unity and perspective

~~died two weeks later.~~ *As*
we were walking out to the
parking lot, I kept looking
back, knowing even then
that I would never see him
again.

— adds a few more details to enhance the response to the experience.

151

Here, then, is the edited version as it was rewritten:

I will always remember my visit to the hospital
to see my grandfather. It was a hot, July afternoon. My mother, grandmother, and I drove in our
old un-airconditioned Buick; I remember my legs
sticking to the vinyl-covered seats. My mother
was crying, but she was trying hard not to let me
see her. When we finally got to the hospital we
found out that children under ten were not permitted in the patients' rooms. I was upset. I was
supposed to see him, I thought. Why couldn't I?
I waited in the lobby where a skinny old security
guard watched my every move. His pants bagged as
he shuffled back and forth across the room. The
hospital was busy; people in white smocks were
darting around. I was scared by the noise and the
mean security guard constantly watching me.
Confined to the couch, I became very bored. About
an hour later my mother and grandmother, both with
sullen faces, came out of my grandfather's room
and walked to the desk. Ignoring the guard, I
walked to the desk and talked to Mom. Crying, she
explained that Grandpa was doing well, but I still
could not see him. As we were walking out to the

parking lot, I kept looking back, knowing even
then that I would never see him again.

After studying the revised version, the student made a few
changes for the final draft:

indent →

I will always remember my visit

to the hospital to see my

grandfather. It was *on* a hot,

July afternoon. My mother,

grandmother, and I drove in

our old un-airconditioned Buick;

I remember my legs sticking

(as the dry wind kept hitting my face
to the vinyl-covered seats.*)*

—more details about trip

My mother was crying, but she

was trying hard ~~not~~ to *hide it* ~~let me~~

~~see her~~. When we finally got

to the hospital, we *were told* ~~found out~~

that children under ten were

not permitted in the patients'

rooms. I was upset. I was

supposed to see him, I thought.

- be more aware of chronology here

Just because I was
Why couldn't I? ∧ I ~~waited~~ in ~~sat~~
only six? Mother told me I would have to ~~wait~~
the lobby where a skinny old

security guard watched my every

move. His pants bagged as he

- adds personal comment

shuffled back and forth across

Boy, he sure didn't like kids
the room. ∧ The hospital was

busy; people in white smocks

were darting around. I was

scared by the noise and the

mean security guard constantly

watching me. Confined to the

and fidgety
couch, I became very bored. ∧

About an hour later my mother

and grandmother, both with

sullen faces, came out of my

grandfather's room and walked

to the desk. Ignoring the

who yelled something

guard, I ~~walked to the desk~~

ran over

~~and talked~~ to Mom. Crying,

—add another verb for sequencing

she explained that Grandpa was

doing well, but I still could

not see him. As we were walk-

on that hot, July day

ing out to the parking lot, I

"If he was doing well, why couldn't I? I still didn't understand."

kept looking back, knowing even

got to

then that I would never see

him ~~again~~.

After studying the revised version, the student made a few
more changes and submitted this essay:

I will always remember my visit to the hospital

to see my grandfather. It was on a hot, July after-

noon. My mother, grandmother, and I drove in our
old, un-airconditioned Buick; and I remember my
legs sticking to the vinyl-covered seats as the
dry wind kept hitting my face. My mother was
crying, but she was trying hard to hide it. When
we finally got to the hospital, we were told that
children under ten were not permitted in the
patients' rooms. I was upset. I was supposed to
see him, I thought. Why couldn't I? Just because
I was only six? Mother told me I would have to
wait in the lobby. I resisted a little, but
finally gave in. So there I sat in the lobby where
a skinny old security guard watched my every move.
His pants bagged as he shuffled back and forth
across the room. Boy, he sure didn't like kids.
The hospital was busy; people in white smocks
darted around everywhere. I was scared by the
noise and the mean security guard constantly
watching me. Confined to the couch, I became very
bored and fidgety. About an hour later, my mother
and grandmother, both wil sullen faces, came out
of my grandfather's room and walked to the nurses'
desk. Ignoring the guard, who had yelled something
at me, I bolted out of my seat and ran over to

my mom. Crying, she explained that Grandpa was
doing well, but I could not see him. If he was
doing well, why couldn't I? I still didn't understand. As we were walking out to the parking lot
on that hot, July day, I kept looking back, knowing
even then that I would never get to see him.

PART V
WRITING
RESEARCH
PAPERS

The *research paper*—sometimes called a library paper, documented paper, or term paper—differs from the other types of writing discussed in this text in two significant ways: first, it requires you to do research, to find facts to support the ideas that you are developing; second, it requires you to follow an approved procedure in documenting those facts so that your reader will know your sources.

With these two exceptions, and with the possible exception that a research paper is also likely to be longer than many of your other writing projects, research writing is actually no different from the other types of writing you have been doing. In it, you present a thesis to prove; you use one of the three orders of organization to arrange your materials; and you make use of one or more of the modes of development for thinking through your ideas.

You may have a problem shared by many other students with research writing: you may fail to see the parts because you are frightened of the whole. If you become intimidated by the prospect of "a fully documented paper due four weeks from today," you may not see how easily you can break the project down into its parts and work on one thing at a time.

You should realize that writing a research paper is divided into five broad steps. If you take each step in the order discussed here and complete each step before moving to the next, you will avoid many of the problems which otherwise might frustrate you. Here are the five steps:

1. Carefully select a topic
2. Prepare a working bibliography
3. Read and take notes
4. Organize notes and write the rough draft
5. Prepare the final copy, including documentation

1. CAREFULLY SELECT A TOPIC

The suggestions for limiting a topic that appear in Part IV *(2B)* also apply to the research paper, but there are some other, special considerations you need to observe:

A. BE INTERESTED

You should select a topic in which you are genuinely interested. Remember that you are going to "live with" your research topic for some time; you do not want to be bored. In most instances your instructor will assign broad topic areas. It is then your turn to focus that broad area to a special segment of the topic about which you are or can become interested.

BROAD TOPIC	FOCUSED AND LIMITED TOPIC
World War II	How conscientious objectors were treated during World War II
Curriculum changes in elementary schools	How the teaching of math at elementary schools in Johnson County has changed since 1975
The poetry of William Wordsworth	How Wordsworth projects attitudes toward nature in his poetry

B. BE ORIGINAL

Avoid a topic about which there is probably little new to say. If you take a tired, overworked topic like capital punishment or abortion, you will probably write a tired, boring paper that says things already said in several hundred other papers.

C. BE UNBIASED

Avoid a topic about which you have a strong opinion before you begin your research. The purpose of research is first to find facts and then to analyze those facts to reach a conclusion. If you go into your research believing, for instance, that all conscientious objectors were treated unjustly during World War II, you will probably look for evidence to support your view and neglect all other evidence. It is a good idea to phrase your research topic as a question and then to answer that question.

D. BE PRAGMATIC

Avoid a topic for which you cannot readily find the necessary source materials. You do not want to select a topic only to find that there are no books or magazine articles available on your subject. Even though there might be excellent material across town at another library or available through interlibrary loan, you may not have time to obtain this material. So before you fix on a topic, be certain that a reasonable amount of source material is at hand in your own library.

The material on preparing a preliminary bibliography *(see 2E)* provides some suggestions about preliminary reading. Review this section and use it as a guide as you review your library's holdings on materials related to your topic.

Unless your instructor has assigned you a topic, it is a good idea, especially in the early stages, to remain somewhat flexible about your topic. As you begin your library search, be open to possibilities of expanding your topic and, similarly, to possibilities of further restricting it.

2. PREPARE A WORKING BIBLIOGRAPHY

A. FINDING LIBRARY MATERIALS

To make effective use of the resources in your library, you should learn how to locate the books and periodicals that will help you in your research.

The first place to look for material on your topic is in the library's card catalog. This file contains three types of cards—author, title, and subject—for every book in the library.

Checking the card catalog for a particular book, however, is using only part of the information available from this valuable source. Learn to read the cards carefully to gather other information which might help you to evaluate the book itself or lead you to headings that will contain other sources.

One part of the card lists brief comments about the contents of the book. Learning to scan these comments quickly and to interpret them can often give you clues to the worth of the book. From these comments you can learn which content areas the book includes and whether or not it contains illustrations (charts, maps, graphs) or a bibliography — which can be very important in helping you find other source materials.

Another part of the catalog card lists the subject headings under which the book is listed. Perhaps you have not thought of all possible alternate headings for your topic. Studying these subject headings can often give you ideas of other places in the card catalog where you might find information on your topic.

A representative author card from the card catalog is shown on p. 164.

B. USING REFERENCE BOOKS

Libraries maintain a large number of reference books, including atlases, biographical dictionaries, unabridged and special-interest dictionaries, general and specialized bibliographies, encyclopedias, and yearbooks.

Some of these reference books provide useful resource material. For instance, you might get an overview of your topic by reading about it in an encyclopedia, or you might quickly learn about important persons by reading about them in one of the *Who's Who* books. For the most part, though, these books will provide you with the names of authors and the

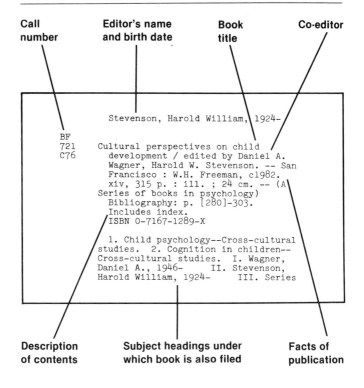

Call number — Editor's name and birth date — Book title — Co-editor

```
            Stevenson, Harold William, 1924-
   BF
   721    Cultural perspectives on child
   C76       development / edited by Daniel A.
             Wagner, Harold W. Stevenson. -- San
             Francisco : W.H. Freeman, c1982.
             xiv, 315 p. : ill. ; 24 cm. -- (A
          Series of books in psychology)
             Bibliography: p. [280]-303.
             Includes index.
             ISBN 0-7167-1289-X

             1. Child psychology--Cross-cultural
          studies.  2. Cognition in children--
          Cross-cultural studies.  I. Wagner,
          Daniel A., 1946-      II. Stevenson,
          Harold William, 1924-      III. Series
```

Description of contents — Subject headings under which book is also filed — Facts of publication

In addition to the name of the author and the title of the book, look at the other potentially helpful information available to you on this card. You learn that the book has a bibliography, which may direct you to other source materials. You might also want to check the subject headings under which it is cross-referenced for other sources. And you might want to see if the two editors, Stevenson and Williams, have written any other books on this topic.

titles of other possible resource materials. They can be especially useful in directing you to specific periodical articles which relate to your research topic.

One of the best ways to acquaint yourself with reference books is to spend time browsing through your library's reference collection. There you will see the wide range of books available and find those of special interest to you. A list of reference books is often available from your library's service desk.

The standard reference to reference books is Eugene P. Sheehy's *Guide to Reference Books.* This excellent source lists reference books under subject classifications and annotates them. For instance, if you are researching in the general area of economics, you will find all the useful reference books on economics listed in Sheehy's book.

C. USING A COMPUTER SEARCH

More and more libraries are linking themselves with specialized information networks which provide bibliographic information through computer terminals. Using a computer search can save you hours of time that you would otherwise spend working your way through reference books, guides, and card catalogs. Nevertheless, computer research is not quite so simple as that. You need some special training in how to phrase your broad and limited topic to enter it into the computer system. If you do not use the proper language, you will not get complete results. Also, most libraries charge from $5 to $75 for a computer search.

Most undergraduate research can be conducted without computer searches. Such searches often provide far more infor-mation than you would have time to read and use for an undergraduate paper. If you have any questions about the value of computer search for your topic, talk with your librarian.

D. EVALUATING YOUR SOURCES

Certainly you want to find a large number of **potential** sources for your research. However, you should not blindly use everything you find just because it relates in some way to your topic. Here are some criteria to help you evaluate individual sources.

Recent Sources

Be certain to use the most recent sources pertinent to your topic. An article written in 1958 may be badly outdated now. You should also recognize that some books and articles are definitive studies in their fields and must be cited regardless of publication dates. Because it is necessary to use recent sources, it is imperative that you consult periodicals for materials. Most books take from one to three years to write and publish, which obviously makes them dated by the time they are published.

Standard Sources

Be certain that you have used the standard sources, the most important scholars recognized in this field. As you read about your topic, you are likely to find some name or title mentioned again and again. The fact that you are seeing this name or title in a variety of different places suggests that you should become familiar with the author or the work. If you were writing a research paper on William Faulkner, you would be expected to refer to the work of Edmond Volpe, one of the most respected Faulkner scholars. If you were writing a paper on techniques for dog training, you would want to consult the work of Barbara Wodehouse, the currently popular authority in this field.

Reliable Sources

Be certain that your sources are reliable. Remember that not everything you read is true and not everything is free of bias. Some authors have acquired reputations for deliberately manipulating, even inventing, their facts to tilt arguments in their favor. Some authors have a strong bias which they openly admit; they make no pretense of examining both sides of an issue. Some publishers, especially publishers of magazines and pamphlets, are cause oriented; everything they publish supports one of their causes: reduction of taxes, equality of the sexes, racial pride, a specific religious point of view. If you elect to use material from one of these cause-oriented sources, you must also take care to seek out an opposing viewpoint as a balance.

You should avoid the mistake of going directly to the library and beginning to read and take notes on your topic. First, spend some time doing preliminary reading. That is, examine your library's holdings to see what is available on your topic. As you discover material, make bibliography cards *(see E)* while the information is before you.

At this stage, do not read in detail all the material you are finding. Instead, do three things: (1) check to see if the material is available in your library; (2) make a bibliography card; and (3) write on that card a brief, general notation about the nature of the work: does it look like something you will want to read later? does it examine only a tiny aspect of your topic? does it appear biased in one way or another?

167

These notes will be helpful to you later because they will give you valuable guidelines for using your time — tell you what information is most useful, what you might want only to scan, and what you might be able to ignore.

E. BIBLIOGRAPHY CARDS

Make bibliography cards for material you think will be useful. These cards will be invaluable aids to you as you write your paper and prepare your final bibliography. In fact, although you need not follow the final bibliography format *(see 5F)* on these cards, you will save yourself time later if you work closely to that form in the early stages.

Most writers use either 3-by-5 inch or 4-by-6 inch index cards for their bibliography cards. Whichever you use, remember that you must make a separate card for **each** source you discover. Even if they are from the same author, do not place two sources on the same card.

The following information should be included on a bibliography card for a book:

Name(s) of author(s)

Reverse the name of the author (**Smith, John** instead of **John Smith**); if more than one author, reverse the name of the first author only.

Title of book

Underlined

City of publication

Publisher's name

Publication date

Library call number

Your own brief comment about the contents of the book

168

The following information should be on a bibliography card for a magazine or journal article:

Name(s) of author(s)
In the same format as noted above for a book

Title of article

In quotation marks

Title of magazine or journal

Underlined

Volume number

Date of publication

Inclusive page numbers of article

Your own brief comment about the contents of the article

Two sample bibliography cards, one for a book and another for an article in a journal, are shown on pages 170 and 171.

3. READ AND TAKE NOTES

As you read the various books and magazines you find, you should begin systematically taking notes on the information you feel will be useful as you write your paper. Do not simply mark the page or write yourself a note to reread page 433 in Dobbs. Rather, take time, while you are reading the material and while you are impressed with its worth, to make a note card.

Note cards can be any size, but most writers use 4-by-6 inch cards. You might find it convenient to use 3-by-5 cards for your bibliography and 4-by-6 for notes; in this way you will not confuse sources and notes or misfile either.

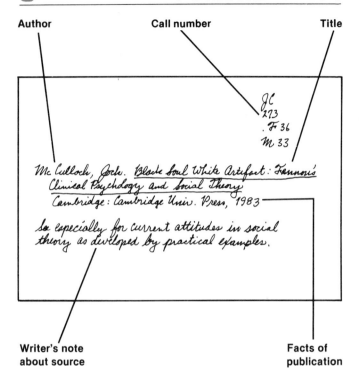

Author   **Call number**   **Title**

Writer's note   **Facts of**
about source   **publication**

At first, taking notes may seem time consuming. However, you should not short-circuit the procedure. Taking good notes **while you are reading** can save you hours of writing time when you sit down to write the complete paper. Many of your notes can be worked into the paper in exactly or almost exactly the form you have written on your note cards.

Place only one note on each card. One of the major reasons for taking notes on cards is to provide you with flexibility in organizing your final paper. At that point you can rearrange your note cards, putting them in the sequence you think

Journal title **Author** **Article title**

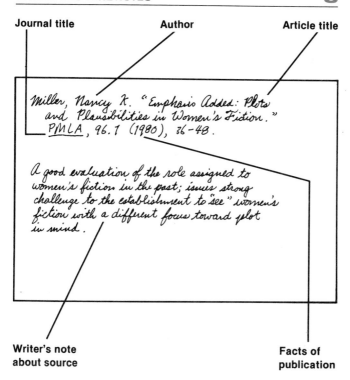

Miller, Nancy K. "Emphasis Added: Plots and Plausibilities in Women's Fiction." _PMLA_, 96.1 (1980), 36-48.

A good evaluation of the role assigned to women's fiction in the past; issues strong challenge to the establishment to "see" women's fiction with a different focus toward plot in mind.

Writer's note about source **Facts of publication**

works best for the finished paper. If you have two separate ideas on the same card, you cannot organize easily.

Every note card must have the following:

1. Author's last name (If you have two or more sources with the same author's last name, use her or his last name followed by one or two key words from the title).
2. Page(s) from which you have taken this information.
3. The note itself.

You will also find it useful to place short labels or headings on your notes as you make them. You may, for example, realize that a particular bit of information belongs in your historical background section and another in your section on current attitudes. By writing "historical backgrounds" or "current attitudes" at the tops of those cards, you are already beginning to piece your paper together. If you have developed a tentative working outline at this stage of your reading and note taking, you might try to make your labels fit sections of your outline.

Here is the way one writer made a note card for her philosophy paper on the difference between essence and existence.

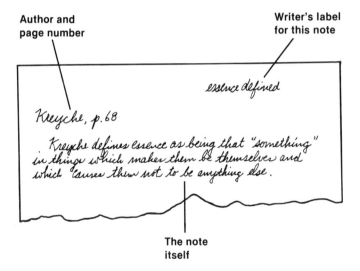

Author and   **Writer's label**
page number   **for this note**

essence defined

Kreyche, p. 68

Kreyche defines essence as being that "something" in things which makes them be themselves and which causes them not to be anything else.

The note
itself

As you take notes, avoid the temptation to make all your notes direct quotations. If you take only quotation notes, you will be tempted later to use too many direct quotations in your final paper. If you do, your paper will look like a cut-and-paste of other people's ideas and will show very little of your own efforts toward synthesizing the various ideas you have considered.

A. SUMMARY NOTES

Most of your notes will summarize original source material. A summary is a general statement, in your own words, of the major ideas from the original. To write a summary note, you must read the original carefully, paying attention to the whole and not the parts, and capture the essence of its meaning, putting the condensed version in your own words. Try not to look at the original as you write your note and be especially careful not to pick up phrases or clauses from the original. Use your own words, remembering that a summary should be shorter than the original. Look at the following paragraph from Rollo May's *The Art of Counseling;* then notice how one student summarized it in his own words:

ORIGINAL

This universal inferiority feeling has its roots in the real inferiority of the infant, who sees the adults around him walking and lifting things and exerting power which he lacks. It is also traceable in part to the real inferiority of primitive man as he strove against animals. Tooth for tooth and claw for claw, man was an easy prey for animals; and hence it was necessary that he compensate for his physical weakness by mental agility. The development of civilization is to be understood to some extent as compensatory; i.e., a result of man's striving to overcome his inferiority.

SUMMARY

Feelings of inferiority can be traced to infants, who feel physically inferior to the adults around them, and to primitive man, who had to fight the wild animals. Man's tendency to use his mental skills to compensate for his physical weaknesses is evidence of inferiority.

B. PARAPHRASE NOTES

If you find material so good that you want to use it in its entirety but do not want to quote directly, you should make a paraphrase note. Unlike a summary, a paraphrase covers all the ideas of the original but puts them into other words.

To paraphrase effectively, you must read carefully to be certain that you understand what the author is really saying; then you must rewrite the passage in your own words. Because the paraphrase is concerned with the details of the original, it may be as long as the original. Here is an original passage from Sigmund Freud's *Jokes and Their Relation to the Unconscious,* followed by a student's paraphrase of that original.

ORIGINAL

We should thus find no difficulty in indicating the aims of any new attempt to throw light on jokes. To be able to count on success, we should have either to approach the work from new angles or to endeavor to penetrate further by increased attention and deeper interest. We can resolve that we will at least not fail in this last respect. It is striking with what a small number of instances of jokes recognized as such the authorities are satisfied for the purposes of their enquiries, and how each of them takes the same ones over from his predecessors.

PARAPHRASE

There should be no problems in our analyzing the objectives of certain efforts to understand jokes. To be successful, we would need to bring a new approach to the problem or try to analyze more intently and more thoroughly. The very few samples of jokes with which the experts are content for their analysis are surprising, as is also the manner in which each expert uses the same jokes as did those who preceded him.

C. DIRECT QUOTATION NOTES

As suggested earlier, you should be wary of taking too many notes as direct quotations. At times, however, the language an author uses will be so powerful that you want to quote it exactly. At other times you will want to quote exactly because the voice of the author lends authority to your statement.

When you do make note cards containing direct quotations, be careful to mark them clearly. You do not want accidentally to present someone else's words as your own when you write the final paper. Place highly visible quotation marks around your note when it is a direct quotation.

Remember also that you do not need to copy every word or phrase from the original. Make use of ellipses *(see II 7)* to eliminate from your quotation those parts of the sentence or paragraph that are not necessary to your report. Look at the way ellipses can be used with sentences from the two previous paragraphs:

". . . you should be wary of taking too many notes as direct quotations."

"At other times . . . the voice of the author lends authority to your argument."

"Place highly visible quotation marks around your note. . . ."

D. PLAGIARISM

Plagiarism is passing someone else's words and original ideas off as your own. At one level, plagiarism is blatantly dishonest. This type of plagiarism occurs when a student submits a paper—borrowed from a friend, bought from a service, or found in a dusty file somewhere—and pretends that the work is his or her own. When this type of dishonesty is discovered — and it is more often than not — the student is usually failed in the course and sometimes dismissed from the school.

Not all plagiarism, however, is this blatant. Sometimes it occurs because students do not realize how closely their work echoes the original source. Remember that you cannot copy a passage, change merely a word here and there, and call the rewritten material your own. A good rule of thumb is to avoid picking up word clusters (phrases or clauses) from sources.

Here is an original passage from Anthony Trollope's essay, "Genius of Hawthorne." The passage which follows, probably intended by the student as a paraphrase, is actually plagiarised because it is too close to the language of the original.

ORIGINAL

Hester sees it too, and her strength, which suffices for the bearing of her own misery, fails her almost to fainting as she understands the condition of the man she has loved. Then there is a scene, the one graceful and pretty scene in the book, in which the two meet—the two who were lovers—and dare for a moment to think that they can escape.

PLAGIARISED

Hester also sees it, and the strength, which is enough for supporting her own misery, leaves her almost to fainting when she becomes aware of the state of the one she has loved. There is also the scene, the only graceful and pretty one in the book, where the two meet—they who were lovers—and dare momentarily to imagine that they can get away.

4. ORGANIZE NOTES AND WRITE THE ROUGH DRAFT

The organizational principles of the research paper are actually no different from those used in any other writing project. Like any other essay, the finished paper will have an introduction, a body, and a conclusion. The major difference is that the research paper may be considerably longer than most freshman essays.

Actually, making the parts hold together will not be an especially difficult task if you remember the following basic tenets of effective writing:

1. Have a clearly stated thesis and make certain that every paragraph develops that thesis.
2. Arrange your ideas in a logical system so that one idea grows naturally out of the other or leads naturally to the next.
3. Provide adequate transition between the parts of your essay so your reader can follow the way you are thinking (writing) and the way you want him or her to think (read).

If you have labeled your note cards, a major part of your organizational task is completed: you already know where most of your material belongs.

If you did not label your note cards as you took them, now is the time to spread them out and supply subtopics. What you are doing in this instance is classifying (see pp. 133–135). If your research topic is **disappearing wildlife in the Midwest,** for instance, you might discover that your note cards can fit into the following categories: **statistics, invasion of territory, hunters, pollution, solutions.**

177

A. OUTLINES

An outline is an organizational guide to help you arrange
your ideas in a logical and thorough manner. Unfortunately,
the concept of the outline has been made unpleasant by some
well-meaning teachers who made it an end rather than a
means to an end. The purpose of an outline is to help you
write, not to get in the way of your writing. If you spend more
time tinkering with your outline — making sure all of the parts fit
together just right — than you do writing your paper, you are
not letting the principle of outlining work for you.

An outline, properly conceived and used, can help you
greatly as you organize your longer research report. It can
enable you to see quickly if there is a logical flow to your ideas
and if you are giving each of your subtopics thorough
coverage.

If you look over the range of possibilities mentioned earlier
for a paper on disappearing wildlife in the Midwest, you
might begin to see several different patterns emerging. You
might write about statistical changes in wildlife population
over the last several years, examine the three problem
areas — invasion of territory, hunters, and pollution — and
then propose some solutions. Perhaps you would discover as
you reread your notes that the animals' territory was invaded to
the largest extent during the late 1950s and early 1960s, and you
might discover that hunting became a greater problem as more
and more people encroached upon the animals' territory. Then
you probably will find that pollution became an especially
significant problem during the late 1960s and throughout the
1970s. As you think about your topic, then, you will begin to
see the emergence of a chronological development. Further,
you might come to recognize that it would be more effective

to layer your statistics into each of the three other areas of development rather than to have one section containing nothing but statistics.

If this becomes your plan, you might come up with a final outline that looks something like this:

I. An overview of the problem
   a. Changing duck population in Lake County
     1. One-third less than in 1955
     2. Nesting grounds destroyed
     3. Overhunted
     4. Killed by pollution
   B. Other endangered species
   C. Public attitude

II. Invasion of territory
   a. Movement from city to country
     1. Many smaller farms
     2. Destruction of nesting and grazing spots
     3. Noise from construction activity and
       automobiles
   B. Building of new superhighways and roads
     1. Destroyed many forested areas
     2. Changed boundaries of some rivers and
       lakes
     3. Noise of heavy construction activities
   C. Statistical changes in population

III. Hunters
    A. A new breed
       1. Greedy
       2. Destructive
       3. Environmentally unaware
    B. Statistical changes in population

IV. Pollution
    A. Water sources
       1. Chemical pollutants
       2. Physical pollutants
    B. Food sources
       1. Chemical pollutants
       2. Physical pollutants
    C. Statistical changes in population

V. Solutions
    A. Citizens' Action Groups
    B. People-free grazing and feeding
       reservations
    C. Stricter hunting laws
    D. Heavier penalties for polluting
       environment

B. THE ROUGH DRAFT

Once you have arranged your ideas and grouped your note cards into the sequences you intend to develop, you are ready to write a rough draft.

Remember that it is an essay, just like any other essay, only longer. If you cannot confront writing the entire paper at one time, write it in sections. If you wrote from the outline given here, for example, you might write the section on invasion of territory one day, the section on hunters the next, and the pollution sequence the day after that. Once you have written all the sections, you can go back through them and provide appropriate transitions to link them together as a part of your editing process.

C. THE INTRODUCTION

The introduction to your research paper should follow the same format as any other introduction. Because a research paper is longer, however, you are likely to devote more space to an attention-getting device *(see IV 4C)*. In the outline given earlier, the writer intends the first section, the overview, to be part of the introduction. Using the information on duck populations will provide a striking or dramatic beginning for the paper.

Sometimes, especially with a longer essay, you may find that it is easier to write the introduction after you have written the body of the essay. After you have written those sequences of the body, you will have a feeling for the whole, a knowledge of what really needs to be said in the introduction, and a sense of the tone of the entire paper.

D. THE BODY

The body of your essay will consist of the supporting ideas and facts you found in your research. Although a research paper is usually longer than other essays, the body is developed in exactly the same manner as are other writing projects.

After you have written the segments of the body of your paper, you must go back through them to see that they hold

together and that you have provided sufficient transition
signals to take the reader along with you.

E. THE CONCLUSION

The conclusion of your research report should be clean and
efficient *(see IV 4E)*. Because your paper itself is long, you
should restate your thesis in the conclusion. If your paper is
designed to call for a specific action (as is the one discussed
above), list in summary fashion those specific actions you want
your reader to take. If you are not calling for a specific action — that is, if your paper is informational — summarize the
significant facts you have discovered through your research;
then let go. Don't drag your conclusion out needlessly.

5. PREPARE THE FINAL COPY, INCLUDING DOCUMENTATION

A. REVISING THE PAPER

The research paper should, of course, go through the same
stages of revision as any other essay *(see IV 5A for a
checklist)*. The length and complexity of the research paper
require that you pay special attention to the flow of ideas.
Make certain that each paragraph does what it is supposed to do
and that the parts of your essay appear in proper sequence.
Once you have the entire paper in front of you, it would not
be unusual for you to rearrange the parts. Do not be afraid to
make such changes if they are necessary.

   After you have arranged the paper into satisfactory order,
read it again for grammatical and mechanical matters. Make

the necessary corrections on your rough draft or on one of your preliminary drafts. Do not put off the editing until you are typing or writing your final copy.

B. INTRODUCING SOURCE INFORMATION

Whether you use direct quotations, paraphrases, or summaries, it is important to introduce your reference materials correctly. The language you use as you introduce a source has a strong impact on your reader.

You should never use a source without introducing it. In the following example, the writer uses a quotation from a book but does not prepare the reader for it:

It becomes obvious, then, that the attitude presently held regarding the farmers of this country must be changed. Unless major changes in the economic perspectives of farming are made, we may find ourselves without farms and farmers. "American economy was built on the farm and, even today, will surely die without it."

This writer simply tags on the quotation at the end of the paragraph. The reader has no lead into the quotation, no hint within the context of the paragraph of the source and its importance.

If you use effective language in introducing a source, you can capture your reader's attention. Look at some of the following techniques:

Recognized Chaucer scholar F. N. Robinson has gone so far as to suggest . . .

According to a recent study completed by Professor Marilyn Franz at the Center for Nuclear Analysis . . .

In his book *Truth and Art,* Albert Hofstadter states . . .

A recent article in *Newsweek* proposes that . . .

You do not need to make such introductions each time you use the same source. Assume that your readers remember the first introduction and have accepted the credibility you attempted to establish there. If subsequent references are presented close to the initial reference, you may need no lead at all. If there have been several intervening references, use leads something like these:

Robinson counters this argument with . . .

Franz also writes . . .

C. MOVING FROM SOURCE INFORMATION

You do not want your paper to be simply a cut-and-paste collection of the works of others. You must show that you have not only read the material you are using but also understood it and brought your own interpretation to it.

Try the technique of "spinning off" from your sources. Introduce information from one of your sources to get an idea, perhaps a paragraph, going. Then spin away from it by offering your own comment or, in some instances, by comparing this position to that found in another source. Look at these examples:

Robinson's argument seems to be fully justified in light of the historical . . .

The position which Franz takes here is directly opposed to the position supported by . . .

D. DOCUMENTING YOUR MATERIAL

As you begin to work toward the final version of your research paper, you must come to terms with the process of documentation. Because you have read material from a large number of sources, you must document those sources.

Your first major concern will be what to document and what not to document. You do not have to document recognized facts or information to which the general public has ready access. You do not have to document that Thomas Paine wrote *Common Sense* or who won last year's World Series. The first is a recognized fact; the second is readily available to anyone who cares to find it.

You are obliged to document facts you have obtained from sources that do not fit into either of the categories given above. You must document all opinions, analyses, interpretations, projections, tables, or charts from your sources; and you must document every direct quotation.

Although beginning research writers sometimes document excessively, you should document any item about which you have question.

E. DOCUMENT FORMATS

Two traditional formats for documenting your work are footnotes and endnotes. In addition to these traditional techniques, many organizations, now including even the conservative Modern Language Association, use in-text documentation.

The following examples represent acceptable formats. Keep in mind that there is no absolutely right way to document. Each discipline, and sometimes each teacher, has particular and sometimes personal, requirements. If you are given directions which differ from the examples below, follow them throughout your paper.

Footnotes

Footnotes are the most conventional form for documenting a research paper. Their major disadvantage is that they are extremely difficult to type so that they fall on the correct page and fill the paper to its proper margins.

If you use footnotes, observe the following conventions:

1. Place an Arabic numeral at the end of the material to be footnoted. Put the numeral outside the punctuation marks and raised slightly above the line.
2. Separate footnotes from the text of your paper with triple spacing or with a twelve-space line typed against the left margin.
3. Announce the beginning of each note with an Arabic numeral corresponding to the numeral in the text. Place the numeral slightly above the line, indented five spaces from the left margin. Subsequent lines of the same note go flush against the left margin.
4. Single space each complete footnote; double space between footnotes.
5. Number your footnotes consecutively throughout the paper.
6. Place footnotes on the same page where the material to which they refer appears in the text.

Endnotes

Endnotes are similar to footnotes except that they appear at the end of the text of your paper. Many of the problems of typing footnotes are eliminated by presenting them as endnotes. If you use endnotes, follow these conventions:

1. Begin your list of notes on a new page, immediately after the final page of the text.
2. Place the title "Notes" or "Reference" on this page, centered, two inches from the top.

3. Do not number the first page of notes; but count it and begin numbering all subsequent pages of your notes consecutively with the paper itself.
4. Single space each complete note and double space between individual notes.

In all other respects, the format of footnotes and endnotes is the same. Both formats correspond to the following examples, the most commonly accepted formats for writing footnotes or endnotes. (Corresponding bibliographic forms for the same material are given on pp. 196–199.)

Books

BOOK WITH ONE AUTHOR

¹E. L. Doctorow, The Book of Daniel (New York: Random House, 1971), p. 233.

In document notes, the author's last name does not appear first as it does in bibliographic form. The facts of publication—city, publisher, and date—are enclosed in parentheses. The document note lists the exact page or pages referred to at this time.

BOOK WITH TWO OR THREE AUTHORS

¹C. Jeriel Howard and Richard Francis Tracz, The Paragraph Book (Boston: Little, Brown and Company, 1982), pp. 45–48.

If you have two authors, separate them with an **and.** If you have three authors, use a comma to separate the first from the second and an **and** to separate the second from the third.

A BOOK WITH MORE THAN THREE AUTHORS

¹Floyd Stovell, et al., Eight American Authors: A Review of Research and Criticism (New York: W. W. Norton & Company, 1963), p. 54.

If you have more than three authors, list the first name and then follow it with the abbreviation et al., meaning "and others."

EDITED BOOK

¹William D. Howells, <u>The Rise of Silas Lapham,</u> ed. Edwin H. Cady (Boston: Houghton Mifflin Company, 1957), pp. 110–112.

CHAPTER OR ESSAY IN A BOOK

¹Frederick J. Hoffman, "Aldous Huxley and the Novel of Ideas," in <u>Forms of Modern Fiction,</u> ed. William Van O'Connor (Bloomington: Indiana University Press, 1962), p. 192.

The documentation note lists the specific page from which the writer has just used an idea. The bibliographic form (see p. 197) lists the inclusive pages of the essay.

A MULTIVOLUME BOOK

¹Milton Cross and David Ewen, <u>The Milton Cross New Encyclopedia of the Great Composers and Their Music,</u> II (New York: Doubleday and Company, 1969), p. 796

Articles

ARTICLE IN A WEEKLY OR MONTHLY MAGAZINE

¹Talbott Strobe, "Again, the World Holds Its Breath," <u>Time,</u> 20 Feb. 1984, p. 15.

The title of the article is in quotation marks; the title of the magazine is underlined.

UNSIGNED ARTICLE IN A WEEKLY OR MONTHLY MAGAZINE

¹"The Talk of the Town," <u>The New Yorker,</u> 6 Feb. 1984, p. 39.

ARTICLE IN A JOURNAL WITH CONTINUOUS PAGINATION

¹Edward P.J. Corbett, "Some Rhetorical Lessons from John Henry Newman," <u>College Composition and Communication,</u> 31 (1980), p. 408.

Because this journal runs its page numbers continuously throughout one entire volume year, you do not need to show an issue number or month/season of publication.

188

ARTICLE IN A JOURNAL WITH SEPARATE PAGINATION

[1]Suzanne Jacobs, "Composing the In-Class Essay: A Case Study of Rudy," College English, 46.1 (1984), p. 37.

The notation 46.1 indicates that this is the forty-sixth volume of this journal and the first issue of that volume. Since this journal begins numbering each issue anew, you have to include either the issue number or the month/season of publication. An alternate correct form would have been
46 (Jan. 1984), p. 37.

ARTICLE IN A NEWSPAPER

[1]"Housing Values Appreciate by Twelve Percent," Yankton Daily News, 16 Jan. 1984.

If this article had been printed with an author's name, that name would obviously have begun the document note. You should not, however, give the page on which the article appears because many papers issue second editions and the article may be moved from one place to another between editions.

ARTICLE IN AN ENCYCLOPEDIA

[1]"Interferon," The Complete Home Encyclopedia, 1980 ed.

If this article had been printed with an author's name, that name would begin the document note. An encyclopedia entry lists only the edition of the encyclopedia, not the specific page number you are citing.

Special Types of Sources

INTERVIEW

[1]Personal interview with Betty Rouse, 21 Dec. 1983.

LECTURE

[1]Alice Haight, "The Computer vs the Humanistic Tradition," Lecture given at Northeastern Illinois University, Chicago, 19 July 1984.

LETTER

[1]Personal letter from Lawrence Maxwell, 7 March 1984.

MIMEOGRAPHED OR PHOTOCOPIED MATERIAL

¹Jane Peterson, "Guidelines for Document Evaluation," Dallas, 1984, (photocopy).

Report

¹Roscoe Finner, "Ways to Achieve Budget Efficiency under Our Present Restraints," Report from the Ad Hoc Fiscal Committee. Chicago: Area North Day Care Center, 1983.

Unpublished Paper

¹Rose Shaw, "The Stamp Act Congress and Its Implications for the Twentieth Century," (unpublished paper).

Second-Reference Notes

The forms given above are the ones you should use the first time you refer to a particular source. You do not need to repeat the entire form each time you refer to the same source.

If you are referring to the same source cited in the note immediately preceding, simply use **Ibid.** (meaning "the same") with the appropriate page number. If the page is identical to the last page cited, you do not need to list the page number either. What you might do in that instance is see if you really need both notes or if you might make only one citation. Look at the following sequence:

¹William Dean Howells, The Rise of Silas Lapham, ed. Edwin H. Cady (Boston: Houghton Mifflin Company, 1957), p. 110.

²Ibid.

³Ibid., p. 112.

If a source mentioned earlier is not the one immediately preceding, you must cite the author and page number. If you have cited more than one work by the same author, you should use a shortened version of the title along with the author's name. Assuming that earlier in your paper you have provided full initial documentation for two Howells novels: *The Rise of Silas Lapham* and *A Modern Instance* along with full documentation for a critical study of Howells by Rudolf Kirk. The following sequence illustrates how second-reference notes might appear:

[7]Howells, Silas, p. 45.

[8]Ibid., p. 92.

[9]Kirk, p. 183.

[10]Howells, Modern, p. 98.

[11]Howells, Silas, p. 145.

[12]Ibid., p. 160.

In-Text Documentation

In-text documentation, sometimes called *parenthetical documentation* or *parenthetical notes,* is certainly the easiest form of documentation to provide. The physical and social sciences have advocated this form of documentation for many years. Beginning in 1984, the Modern Language Association also moved to in-text documentation.

Besides being much easier to type, the in-text format places a source reference immediately next to the information to which it refers, not at the bottom of the page or several pages away in a collection of endnotes. In addition, in-text documentation eliminates the unnecessary duplication of information provided in the bibliography. If a reader wants to learn enough about your source so he or she can go directly to it, that information is still available in the bibliography.

You can see from the following guidelines that the format for in-text documentation is quite simple:

1. Refer to your source by citing author and page number(s). If your source has no author, refer to it by title.
2. Place in-text documentation in parentheses immediately after you have presented the source material.
3. Treat the material in parenthesis as a part of the sentence. That is, place sentence-level punctuation marks after the parentheses. After long, indented quotations, the in-text documentation occurs **after** the final mark of punctuation from the original material. (See p. 5 of model paper for an example.)

Here are two in-text citations:

Another sociologist takes a decidedly different attitude toward the problem, arguing that the political units of society must become the aggressive agents in any type of social remediation (Watkins 214).

According to one recent magazine article ("People Moving People" 47), the great migration from the cities is slowing.

If your source is a direct quotation, place the end quotation marks after the last word, but place the period after your parentheses.

Mims offers convincing evidence that "Lanier believed in the religious value of music. . . . It was [to him] the church of the future" (Mims 144).

Sometimes the in-text citation may work more effectively in another part of the sentence. For instance, if you have introduced the name of your source, the example above might have been written like this:

Mims (144) offers convincing evidence that "Lanier believed in the religious value of music. . . . It was [to him] the church of the future."

Because the author's name is mentioned in the sentence, it is not repeated in the parenthetical note.

If you cite two or more works by the same author, the author's name alone does not identify the specific work cited. In these instances, you must also provide a shortened version of the title. Suppose you are writing about two novels by Rita Mae Brown, *Rubyfruit Jungle* and *Six of One.* Your in-text citations would take this form:

(<u>Rubyfruit</u> 76)

(<u>Six</u> 185)

Content Endnotes

Sometimes you may want to provide your reader with additional information that would interrupt the on-going development of your thesis. This information should be placed in content endnotes.

If you use content endnotes, they should be placed after the last page of the text, just before the bibliography. Title the page "Notes." Do not number the first page, but number the subsequent pages consecutively with the text of the paper.

Mark content endnotes in your text with Arabic numerals a half-space above the normal line of type. Number the notes consecutively throughout the paper. Type the notes themselves as you would type reference footnotes (see pp. 185–186).

Remember that content endnotes are not documentation notes. They are used in the following situations:

1. To identify a major source that you will use throughout your paper

   [1]Milton's poems are cited from the Odyssey edition of Complete Poems and documented in the text by citing short title and line(s).

2. To offer a blanket citation

   [1]On this point also see Wilson (245) and McMasters (46).

3. To suggest additional reading on the same topic

   [1]For an additional study on the role of Vitamin C in the nutrition of the individual, see especially Jenkins and Meredith.

   Note that this type of content note provides "additional" information to what you have used in your text. You must, therefore, include a complete bibliographic reference to Jenkins and Meredith in your formal bibliography.

4. To compare textual commentary with another source

   [1]Cf. Angwin Richards who contends that Thompson is "perhaps the most significant but least understood theorist of his time" (317).

   This type of note is introduced by using the abbreviation Cf., meaning to compare this source with another. Because you make specific reference to the second source here, you must provide a page number.

5. To explain your methods or procedures

   [1]In order to get a valid sampling for my test group, I identified three randomly selected clusters, each set against its own control group.

6. To acknowledge assistance or suggestions

> ¹I am indebted to Professor Joyce Ewing who first sug-
> gested to me the possibility of focusing my research toward
> the smaller population of Clemson rather than toward a
> larger city.

F. PREPARING A BIBLIOGRAPHY

Your last task as you complete the final version of your
research paper is to prepare a bibliography, a formal list of
the sources you used to develop your research project. Some
instructors require that you list only those sources which you
have actually cited in your paper. If this is the case, use the
heading, **Works Cited** or **Selected Bibliography;** otherwise, head this list with the single word **Bibliography.**

Here are some general guidelines for the format of the
bibliography page:

1. Start the Bibliography on a new page immediately after
   the last page of your text (if you used footnotes or in-
   text documentation) or your endnotes.
2. Do not number the first page. Number other pages of
   the bibliography in sequence with the numbering of the
   paper itself.
3. Type the heading two inches from the top of the page
   and center it.
4. Leave four spaces between the heading and the first entry.
5. Double space each entry and double space between
   separate entries.
6. Block the first word of each entry against the left
   margin. Indent subsequent lines of the same entry five
   spaces.

7. Arrange the listings in alphabetical order by author's last name. Alphabetize entries which do not have an author by the first major word of the title.

The material that goes into your formal bibliography is the same material you have recorded on your bibliography (or source) cards. If you were careful to copy all the information correctly in making those cards, writing the formal bibliography means merely arranging each entry and the proper format.

Sample Bibliography Forms

Here are some examples of the types of entries you will most often need to use:

Books

BOOK WITH ONE AUTHOR

Doctorow, E. L. The Book of Daniel. New York: Random House, 1971.

List the author's name exactly as it appears on the title page of the book. Use initials if they are used there; use full names if they are used there.

BOOK WITH TWO OR THREE AUTHORS

Howard, C. Jeriel, and Richard Francis Tracz. The Paragraph Book. Boston: Little, Brown and Company, 1982.

Only the first author's name is reversed. In a book with three authors, a comma separates the first and second author and a comma followed by an **and** separates the second and third authors. List the publisher's name in exactly the format used on the title page, abbreviating only words that are abbreviated there.

BOOK WITH MORE THAN THREE AUTHORS

Stovall, Floyd, et al. Eight American Authors: A Review of Research and Criticism. New York: W.W. Norton & Company, 1963.

List the first author's name and follow it with the abbreviation et al., meaning "and others." Notice that the subtitle of a book is always separated from the title by a colon even though there may be no punctuation or a different form of punctuation used on the library card.

TWO OR MORE BOOKS BY THE SAME AUTHOR

Faulkner, William. Absalom, Absalom! New York: Random House, 1951.

———. Sanctuary. New York: Random House, 1959.

For the second and subsequent entries by the same author, use a line composed of seven underscores followed by a period. The works themselves may be arranged in alphabetical order or in chronological order by publication date.

EDITED BOOK

Howells, William D. The Rise of Silas Lapham. Ed. Edwin H. Cady. Boston: Houghton Mifflin Company, 1957.

CHAPTER OR ESSAY IN A BOOK

Hoffman, Frederick J. "Aldous Huxley and the Novel of Ideas." In Forms of Modern Fiction. Ed. William Van O'Connor. Bloomington: Indiana University Press, 1962, pp. 189–200.

The title of the chapter or essay is enclosed within quotation marks; the title of the entire book is preceded by the word **In.** The final part of the listing indicate the pages where the full essay or chapter can be found.

MULTIVOLUME BOOK

Cross, Milton and David Ewen. The Milton Cross New Encyclopedia of the Great Composers and Their Music. Vol. II. New York: Doubleday and Company, 1969.

Articles

ARTICLE IN A WEEKLY OR MONTHLY MAGAZINE

Strobe, Talbott. "Again, the World Holds Its Breath." Time, 20 Feb.
    1984 pp. 14–15.

The title of the article is in quotation marks; the title of the magazine is
underlined. The magazine title is followed by the date of publication (months
with names more than four letters long are usually abbreviated) and the inclusive
page numbers.

UNSIGNED ARTICLE IN A WEEKLY OR MONTHLY MAGAZINE

"The Talk of the Town." The New Yorker, 6 Feb. 1984, pp. 37–41.

Alphabetize the entry according to the title of the article.

ARTICLE IN A JOURNAL WITH CONTINUOUS PAGINATION

Corbett, Edward P. J. "Some Rhetorical Lessons from John Henry
    Newman." College Composition and Communication, 31 (1980),
    pp. 402–412.

Some journals paginate continuously throughout a volume year. In these
instances, it is not necessary to give the issue number or the month of
publication.

ARTICLE IN A JOURNAL WITH SEPARATE PAGINATION

Jacobs, Suzanne, "Composing the In-Class Essay: A Case Study
    of Rudy." College English, 46.1 (1984), pp. 34–42.

The figure 46.1 indicates the forty-sixth volume and the first issue of that
volume. Since this journal begins pagination anew with every issue, either
the issue number or the month/season of publication must be shown. An
alternate correct form is 46 (January, 1984) pp. 34–42.

ARTICLE IN A NEWSPAPER

"Housing Values Appreciate by Twelve Percent." Yankton Daily
    News, 16 Jan. 1984.

If the article is signed, the writer's name appears first in the bibliography entry.
Because some newspapers print several editions on one day, do not give
page numbers because an article can be moved from one edition to another.

ARTICLE IN AN ENCYCLOPEDIA

"Interferon," The Complete Home Encyclopedia, 1980 ed.

Since all articles in an encyclopiedia are alphabetized, you need not show page references. If an article is signed by a specific writer, use that individual's name for the author part of your entry.

Special Types of Sources

INTERVIEW

Rouse, Betty. Personal interview. 21 Dec. 1983.

LECTURE

Haight, Alice. "The Computer vs the Humanistic Tradition." Lecture given at Northeastern Illinois University. Chicago, 19 July 1984.

LETTER

Maxwell, Lawrence. Letter to author. 7 March 1984.

MIMEOGRAPHED OR PHOTOCOPIED MATERIAL

Peterson, Jane. "Guidelines for Document Evaluation." Dallas, 1984. Photocopy.

REPORT

Finney, Roscoe. "Ways to Achieve Budget Efficiency under Our Present Restraints." Report from the Ad Hoc Fiscal Committee. Chicago: Area North Day Care Center, 1983.

UNPUBLISHED PAPER

Shaw, Rose. "The Stamp Act Congress and Its Implications for the Twentieth Century. Unpublished paper.

G. NEW MLA GUIDELINES

In 1984, the Modern Language Association issued a set of guidelines for preparing bibliographies to accompany in-text

documentation. These guidelines have been followed in the
second version of the paper presented in Section *6A*. As you
can see, they differ from the guidelines given in Section *5E*
in two ways:

1. In references to books, only the first word of the
   publisher's name is given. For example "Little, Brown
   & Company" becomes "Little"; and "The Macmillan
   Company" becomes "Macmillan." University Press is
   shortened to UP so that, for example, "Harvard
   University Press" becomes "Harvard UP."
2. In references to periodicals, there is no punctuation
   between the name of the journal and the volume
   number; but there is always a colon at the end of
   whatever precedes the page numbers no matter what
   this material may be.

Because these changes represent a considerable departure from
tradition, it is likely to be some years before they are accepted
everywhere. If you are writing a research paper in English (or
for any other language), you should check with your instructor
to find out whether he or she prefers traditional bibliographical
style or the new MLA style.

6. A SAMPLE RESEARCH PAPER

On the following pages you can study the same
research paper shown in two different formats. In its first
format, the paper has endnote documentation. In its second,
the same paper has in-text documentation.

JOHN QUINCY ADAMS:

ARCHITECT OF NON-INTERVENTION POLICY

David Samuels

Winter Term, 1984

America's present foreign policy has evolved into a complex array of networks, organizations, and treaties. Today, the United States plays a large and significant role in affairs around the globe. This country's president, along with dozens of other diplomats, devotes almost as much energy to problems in other countries as to problems at home, but such has not always been the case. During the early years of this nation, the feeling was much more one of "We'll leave you alone and you leave us alone." Many of our early political leaders, including even George Washington, indicated that the United States should never involve itself in in the affairs of other countries.[1]

One of the principal architects of the non-intervention policy was John Quincy Adams, who was, indeed, the shaping influence behind the Monroe Doctrine, first announced on December 2, 1823. The first major foreign policy statement of the new United States, the Monroe Doctrine addressed three issues: non-colonization, non-intervention, and neutrality toward Europe. While Adams's thinking contributed to both the philosophy and language of all three

3

parts of the doctrine, it was the concept of non-
intervention that required his most careful political maneuvering between opposing forces.[2]

Adams, feeling neutrality was beneficial, echoed
George Washington's plea that the United States
should not enter into any permanent alliances with
any part of the world. His cogent arguments for
a unilateral statement played both upon the new
pride and strength of the United States and upon
latent hostilities to anything European.[3] It was
his rational voice which dissuaded those members
of Congress who wanted to make the Monroe Doctrine
a joint policy statement with Great Britain.

As a writer in his early career, Adams stated
that "impartial and unequivocal neutrality" was
the best policy for the new country.[4] He also
denounced the impressment of Americans by both the
French and the English during their war of 1793.
He extolled America's neutrality in that conflict,
saying we are neutral "as the citizens of a nation at
a vast distance from the continent of Europe; of a
nation whose happiness consists in a real independence, disconnected from all European interests and

4

European politics."[5] Although many people at
this time wanted to support France, Adams pointed
out that such a position would mean supporting
repression in the West Indies and thereby would
solidify the opposition of certain other countries
toward the United States.

Since his first trip to Europe when he was fourteen, Adams had disliked both Europe and the European way of life.[6] Throughout his long political
career, he firmly held the attitude that there were
two political systems--American and European--and
he believed they should be kept apart. In a letter
to Henry Middleton, American ambassador to Russia,
Adams had written that the two systems should be
kept distinct and separate. He believed that "It is
our duty to remain the peaceful and silent, though
sorrowful spectators of the European scene."[7]

When the South American countries first declared
independence, Adams advised Ambassador Richard Rush
to indicate that the United States would be neutral.
Adams, however, subsequently came to realize the
possible benefits of taking a stand on this issue.
While he certainly wanted to remain neutral on

5

European affairs, he also felt that the two systems,
European and Latin American, were separate; therefore
he felt justified in recognizing those emerging
republics. His main goal was to keep the Europeans,
all Europeans, out of the Western Hemisphere.[8]

It was at this very time that Adams perceived a
real threat from the newly formed Holy Alliance,
whose principal members were France and Russia.
France had invaded Spain in order to restore King
Ferdinand VII, and there were rumors of a plan
to regain Spain's lost colonies in the New World.
In each instance where the Holy Alliance, guided
by its doctrine of intervention, moved in to quell
a revolution, the previous system of autocratic
rule was quickly reinstated.[9] The possibility of
French troops being sent to retake Spanish America
and rule autocratically caused much concern in both
the United States and the United Kingdom. In their
summation of the situation, historians Hicks and
Mowry write the following:

> To England the possibility that the Spanish-
> American republics might be restored to Spain
> was alarming, for such a development would

mean in all probability the revival of the
old colonial trade barriers and the consequent
restriction of English trade. Moreover, if
France should help subdue Spanish America,
she could hardly be expected to do it for
nothing. What pay could Ferdinand give other
than an American colony for France?[10]

Britain, in order to try to protect her newfound
trading partners in South America, approached the
the United States ambassador and suggested making
a joint statement against any involvement of the
Holy Alliance in South America. Britain, an early
member of the Alliance, had withdrawn, Lord
Castlereagh calling the Alliance "sublime nonsense."[11]

The British government moved quickly and effi-
ciently to try to persuade the United States to
join her in a joint announcement of foreign policies. Actually, Britain had nowhere else to go to
try restoring the balance of power. After the
Congress of Verona in 1822, at which the Holy
Alliance discussed sending troops to America,
George Canning, the British foreign minister, suggested that the "United States and Great Britain

take concerted steps to block such intervention".[12]

During much of 1823, Canning conducted his personal public relations campaign, designed to appeal
to American diplomats. On April 16 he praised the
American position of neutrality in his address to
the House of Commons. Also, he applauded vigorously
Ambassador Rush's toast "To the success of neutrals!"
Canning subsequently convinced Parliament to repeal
the Foreign Enlistments Act, which had permitted
impressment, in order to show neutrality and amicability toward the United States. Bemis quotes a
dinner speech in which Adams boasted, "The force
of blood again prevails, and the daughter and the
mother stand together against the world."[13]

Largely because of Canning's efforts, negotiations began on the joint statement. Britain,
however, was not ready to acknowledge the independence of the South American republics, and, after a
while, Canning's enthusiasm for the joint statement
cooled. At about this same time, Rush became suspicious of possible ulterior motives on the part of
the British. In his detailed analysis of efforts
toward the joint statement, Professor Bemis sug-

gests that Rush finally "concluded [that] Great Britain was more interested in balancing and holding down European power than in protecting the liberties of Latin America."[14] In relation to Britain's real policy, Rush finally stated, "It is France that must not be aggrandized, not South America that must be made free."[15]

Unknown at that time to United States diplomats, Canning had begun to hold secret meetings with French officials, telling them that Britain would not allow France to take advantage of the situation in South America. When the French assured him that they did not intend to intervene there, he seemed content to let the matter drop. However, communication difficulties of that time prevented information regarding the French position from reaching Washington.[16]

Although President Monroe was originally in favor of a double agreement, Adams remained "suspicious" of the British and urged that the United States operate alone.[17] Even though Monroe was able to draw support for a joint statement from such leaders as Thomas Jefferson and James Madison, Adams remained

9

firm in his opposition.[18]   When it became obvious
that Canning was no longer aggressively attempting
to negotiate a joint statement, Monroe finally
moved to support Adams and his demand for a unilateral statement.[19]

A part of Adams's thinking at this time was shaped
by what he perceived as future roles for Texas and
Cuba. While he did not want to annex those territories outright, he felt that eventually they both
would "gravitate" toward union with the United
States. He feared that a joint agreement made with
Great Britain would not leave the United States
free to accept those territories.[20]

In addition, Adams especially did not want Cuba
to be transferred to Great Britain. The Holy Alliance might have given it to the British in order
to appease them and to allow for their involvement
in an invasion of Latin America by the alliance.
Adams felt quite strongly about this, saying that
the transfer of Cuba to Great Britain "would be an
event unpropitious to the interests of this Union."[21]
Great Britain was equally adamant in its opposition toward Cuba's possible affiliation with the

United States, fearing especially a loss of trade
with Cuba if she became a state. At the Cabinet
meeting of November 7, 1823, Adams gave his reasons
for opposing the joint statement. He was first
suspicious of British sincerity in stopping the
Holy Alliance. More likely, he felt, Britain was
afraid that the United States would acquire new
territories in Latin America. He restated his feeling that Texas and Cuba might themselves want to
become states at some time in the future. He argued
that a joint agreement with Britain would "give her
a substantial and inconvenient pledge against ourselves, and really obtain nothing in return." He
further urged that "We should at least keep ourselves
free to act as emergencies may arise, and not tie
ourselves down to any principle which might immediately afterwards be brought to bear against
ourselves."[22]

   Adams asked what might happen if the Holy
Alliance invaded and Britain defended the colonies.
If Britain won, might new British colonies then
arise? And what exactly were Britain's motives?
She surely did not need the tiny United States navy

to extend her influence.[23]   "It would be more
candid," Adams summarized, "as well as more dignified, to avow our principles explicitly to Russia
and France, than to come in as a cock-boat in the
wake of a British man-of-war."[24]

And so, in the end, because of fears of British
involvement here and because Adams convinced
American diplomats that a joint statement would
be against United States interests, this country
made an independent statement against any involvement of foreign powers in any part of America. The
non-intervention policy gave the new nation "exactly what it most needed, isolation and time to expand
its frontiers to the Pacific, to develop its farms
and factories, to nurture its strength." And,
according to the University of Wisconsin historian
Merle Curti, it was the voice of John Quincy Adams
that crystallized "the national foreign policy which
President Monroe incorporated" into the now famous
Monroe Doctrine.[25]

Historian M. B. Hecht asserts that Adams, with a
"fine intuitive sense" established "with more than
usual brilliance" to both Britain and the Holy

12

Alliance an area (the Western Hemisphere) that would be free from their policies.[26] It was Adams who did the "divining, sensing, seizing, adapting, and combining, at just the right moment in history" to produce "the most significant of all American state papers."[27]

NOTES

¹Dexter Perkins, <u>Hands Off</u>, (Boston: Little, Brown, 1941), p. 17.

²Evelyn Russell, "John Adams as a Politician," <u>Southern Historic Review</u>, 22 (1982), p. 316.

³Marie B. Hecht, <u>John Quincy Adams</u>: <u>A Personal History of an Independent Man</u>, (New York: Macmillan, 1972), p. 264.

⁴John Quincy Adams, <u>The Adams Chronicles</u>, ed. Jack Shepherd (Boston: Little, Brown, 1975), p. 172.

⁵Hecht, p. 264.

⁶Perkins, p. 28.

⁷Samuel Flagg Bemis, <u>John Quincy Adams and the Foundations of American Foreign Policy</u>, (New York: Alfred A. Knopf, 1949), p. 364.

⁸Bemis, p. 255.

⁹Harold Elkins, " The Holy Alliance and a Young Democracy," <u>American Perspective</u>, 39.2 (1978), 87.

¹⁰John D. Hicks and George E. Mowry, <u>A Short History of American Democracy</u>, (Boston: Houghton Mifflin, 1956), p. 197.

¹¹Adams, <u>Chronicles</u>, p. 272.

¹²Henry Steele Commager and Allan Nevins, <u>The Pocket History of the United States</u>, (New York: Pocket Books, 1951), p. 161.

[13]Bemis, p. 379.

[14]Ibid., p. 380.

[15]Ibid.

[16]Hicks and Mowry, p. 198.

[17]Adams, Chronicles, p. 275.

[18]Commager and Nevins, p. 161.

[19]Hicks and Mowry, p. 198.

[20]Walter LaFeber, John Quincy Adams and American Continental Empire, (Chicago, Quadrangle Books, 1965), p. 128.

[21]John Quincy Adams, The Selected Writings of John Adams and John Quincy Adams, ed. Adrienne Koch and William Beden (New York: Alfred A. Knopf, 1972), p. 378.

[22]Adams, Chronicles, p. 290.

[23]LaFeber, p. 109.

[24]Ibid.

[25]Merle Curti, Williard Thorp, and Carlos Baker, American Issues: The Social Record, (Philadelphia: J. B. Lippincott, 1960), p. 156.

[26]Hecht, p. 369.

[27]Bemis, p. 408.

BIBLIOGRAPHY

Adams, John Quincy. <u>The Adams Chronicles</u>.

    Ed. Jack Shepherd. Boston: Little, Brown, 1975.

    _____. <u>The Selected Writings of John Adams and</u>

    <u>John Quincy Adams</u>. Ed. Adrienne Koch and William

    Beden. New York: Alfred A. Knopf, 1972.

Bemis, Samuel Flagg. <u>John Quincy Adams and the</u>

    <u>Foundations of American Foreign Policy</u>. New

    York: Alfred A. Knopf, 1949.

Commager, Henry Steele, and Allan Nevins. <u>The</u>

    <u>Pocket History of the United States</u>. New

    York: Pocket Books, 1951.

Curti, Merle, Williard Thorp, and Carlos Baker.

    <u>American Issues: The Social Record</u>.

    Philadelphia: J. B. Lippincott, 1960.

Elkins, Harold. "The Holy Alliance and a Young

    Democracy." <u>American Perspective</u>, 39.2

    (1978), 84-92.

Hecht, Marie B. <u>John Quincy Adams: A Personal</u>

    <u>History of an Independent Man</u>. New York:

    Macmillan, 1972.

16

Hicks, John D. and George E. Mowry. <u>A Short
History of American Democracy</u>. Boston:
Houghton Mifflin, 1956.

LaFeber, Walter. <u>John Quincy Adams and American
Continental Empire</u>. New York: Alfred A. Knopf,
1946.

Perkins, Dexter. <u>Hands Off</u>. Boston: Little,
Brown, 1975.

Russell, Evelyn. "John Adams as a Politician."
<u>Southern Historic Review</u>, 22 (1982), 315-324.

<u>JOHN QUINCY ADAMS</u>:

<u>ARCHITECT OF NON-INTERVENTION POLICY</u>

<u>David Samuels</u>

Winter Term, 1984

2

America's present foreign policy has evolved into
a complex array of networks, organizations, and
treaties. Today, the United States plays a large
and significant role in affairs around the globe.
This country's president, along with dozens of
other diplomats, devotes almost as much energy
to problems in other countries as to problems at
home, but such has not always been the case. During
the early years of this nation, the feeling was
much more one of "We'll leave you alone and you leave
us alone." Many of our early political leaders,
including even George Washington, indicated that
the United States should never involve itself in
in the affairs of other countries (Perkins 17).

One of the principal architects of the non-
intervention policy was John Quincy Adams, who was,
indeed, the shaping influence behind the Monroe
Doctrine, first announced on December 2, 1823. The
first major foreign policy statement of the new United
States, the Monroe Doctrine addressed three issues:
non-colonization, non-intervention, and neutrality
toward Europe. While Adams's thinking contributed
to both the philosophy and language of all three

parts of the doctrine, it was the concept of non-
intervention that required his most careful political maneuvering between opposing forces (Russell
316).

Adams, feeling neutrality was beneficial, echoed
George Washington's plea that the United States
should not enter into any permanent alliances with
any part of the world. His cogent arguments for
a unilateral statement played both upon the new
pride and strength of the United States and upon
latent hostilities to anything European (Hecht 264).
It was his rational voice which dissuaded those
members of Congress who wanted to make the Monroe
Doctrine a joint policy statement with Great Britain.

As a writer in his early career, Adams stated
that "impartial and unequivocal neutrality" was
the best policy for the new country (<u>Chronicles</u> 172).
He also denounced the impressment of Americans by
both the French and the English during their war of
1793. He extolled America's neutrality in that
conflict, saying we are neutral "as the citizens of
a nation at a vast distance from the continent of
Europe; of a nation whose happiness consists in a

4

real independence, disconnected from all European
interests and European politics" (Hecht 264).
Although many people at this time wanted to support
France, Adams pointed out that such a position would
mean supporting repression in the West Indies and
thereby would solidify the opposition of certain
other countries toward the United States.

Since his first trip to Europe when he was fourteen, Adams had disliked both Europe and the European way of life (Perkins 28). Throughout his long
political career, he firmly held the attitude that
there were two political systems--American and
European--and he believed they should be kept apart.
In a letter to Henry Middleton, American ambassador
to Russia, Adams had written that the two systems
should be kept distinct and separate. He believed
that "It is our duty to remain the peaceful and
silent, though sorrowful spectators of the European
scene" (Bemis 364).

When the South American countries first declared
independence, Adams advised Ambassador Richard Rush
to indicate that the United States would be neutral.
Adams, however, subsequently came to realize the

5

possible benefits of taking a stand on this issue.
While he certainly wanted to remain neutral on
European affairs, he also felt that the two systems,
European and Latin American, were separate; therefore
he felt justified in recognizing those emerging
republics. His main goal was to keep the Europeans,
all Europeans, out of the Western Hemisphere (Bemis
255).

It was at this very time that Adams perceived a
real threat from the newly formed Holy Alliance,
whose principal members were France and Russia.
France had invaded Spain in order to restore King
Ferdinand VII, and there were rumors of a plan
to regain Spain's lost colonies in the New World.
In each instance where the Holy Alliance, guided
by its doctrine of intervention, moved in to quell
a revolution, the previous system of autocratic
rule was quickly reinstated (Elkins 87). The possibility of French troops being sent to retake
Spanish America and rule autocratically caused much
concern in both the United States and the United
Kingdom. In their summation of the situation, historians Hicks and Mowry write the following:

6

To England the possibility that the Spanish-
American republics might be restored to Spain
was alarming, for such a development would
mean in all probability the revival of the
old colonial trade barriers and the consequent
restriction of English trade. Moreover, if
France should help subdue Spanish America,
she could hardly be expected to do it for
nothing. What pay could Ferdinand give other
than an American colony for France?

(Hicks and Mowry 197)

Britain, in order to try to protect her newfound
trading partners in South America, approached the
the United States ambassador and suggested making
a joint statement against any involvement of the
Holy Alliance in South America. Britain, an early
member of the Alliance, had withdrawn, Lord
Castlereagh calling the Alliance "sublime nonsense"
(Chronicles 272).

The British government moved quickly and effi-
ciently to try to persuade the United States to
join her in a joint announcement of foreign poli-

cies.   Actually, Britain had nowhere else to go to try restoring the balance of power.   After the Congress of Verona in 1822, at which the Holy Alliance discussed sending troops to America, George Canning, the British foreign minister, suggested that the "United States and Great Britain take concerted steps to block such intervention" (Commager and Nevins 161).

During much of 1823, Canning conducted his personal public relations campaign, designed to appeal to American diplomats.   On April 16 he praised the American position of neutrality in his address to the House of Commons.   Also, he applauded vigorously Ambassador Rush's toast "To the success of neutrals!" Canning subsequently convinced Parliament to repeal the Foreign Enlistments Act, which had permitted impressment, in order to show neutrality and amicability toward the United States. Bemis quotes a dinner speech in which Adams boasted, "The force of blood again prevails, and the daughter and the mother stand together against the world" (379).

Largely because of Canning's efforts, negotiations began on the joint statement.   Britain,

8

however, was not ready to acknowledge the independence of the South American republics, and, after a while, Canning's enthusiasm for the joint statement cooled. At about this same time, Rush became suspicious of possible ulterior motives on the part of the British. In his detailed analysis of efforts toward the joint statement, Professor Bemis (380) suggests that Rush finally "concluded [that] Great Britain was more interested in balancing and holding down European power than in protecting the liberties of Latin America." In relation to Britain's real policy, Rush finally stated, "It is France that must not be aggrandized, not South America that must be made free" (quoted in Bemis 380).

Unknown at that time to United States diplomats, Canning had begun to hold secret meetings with French officials, telling them that Britain would not allow France to take advantage of the situation in South America. When the French assured him that they did not intend to intervene there, he seemed content to let the matter drop. However, communication difficulties of that time prevented information regarding the French position from reaching

9

Washington (Hicks and Mowry 198).

Although President Monroe was originally in favor
of a double agreement, Adams remained "suspicious"
of the British and urged that the United States
operate alone (Chronicles 275). Even though Monroe
was able to draw support for a joint statement from
such leaders as Thomas Jefferson and James Madison,
Adams remained firm in his opposition (Commager and
Nevins 161). When it became obvious that Canning
was no longer aggressively attempting to negotiate
a joint statement, Monroe finally moved to support
Adams and his demand for a unilateral statement
(Hicks and Mowry 198).

A part of Adams's thinking at this time was shaped
by what he perceived as future roles for Texas
and Cuba. While he did not want to annex those
territories outright, he felt that eventually they
both would "gravitate" toward union with the United
States. He feared that a joint agreement made with
Great Britain would not leave the United States
free to accept those territories (LaFeber 128).

In addition, Adams especially did not want Cuba
to be transferred to Great Britain. The Holy Alli-

10

ance might have given it to the British in order
to appease them and to allow for their involvement
in an invasion of Latin America by the alliance.
Adams felt quite strongly about this, saying that
the transfer of Cuba to Great Britain "would be an
event unpropitious to the interests of this Union"
(Selected 378). Great Britain was equally adamant
in its opposition toward Cuba's possible affiliation
with the United States, fearing especially a loss
of trade with Cuba if she became a state. At the
Cabinet meeting of November 7, 1823, Adams gave his
reasons for opposing the joint statement. He was
first suspicious of British sincerity in stopping
the Holy Alliance. More likely, he felt, Britain
was afraid that the United States would acquire new
territories in Latin America. He restated his feeling that Texas and Cuba might themselves want to
become states at some time in the future. He argued
that a joint agreement with Britain would "give her
a substantial and inconvenient pledge against ourselves, and really obtain nothing in return." He
further urged that "We should at least keep ourselves
free to act as emergencies may arise, and not tie

11

ourselves down to any principle which might immediately afterwards be brought to bear against
ourselves" (<u>Chronicles</u> 290).

Adams asked what might happen if the Holy
Alliance invaded and Britain defended the colonies.
If Britain won, might new British colonies then
arise? And what exactly were Britain's motives?
She surely did not need the tiny United States navy
to extend her influence (LaFeber 109). "It would
be more candid," Adams summarized, "as well as more
dignified, to avow our principles explicitly to
Russia and France, than to come in as a cock-boat
in the wake of a British man-of-war" (LaFeber 109).

And so, in the end, because of fears of British
involvement here and because Adams convinced
American diplomats that a joint statement would
be against United States interests, this country
made an independent statement against any involvement of foreign powers in any part of America. The
non-intervention policy gave the new nation "exactly what it most needed, isolation and time to expand
its frontiers to the Pacific, to develop its farms
and factories, to nurture its strength." And,

12

according to the University of Wisconsin historian
Merle Curti, it was the voice of John Quincy Adams
that crystallized "the national foreign policy which
President Monroe incorporated" into the now famous
Monroe Doctrine (Curti, Thorp, and Baker 156).

   Historian M. B. Hecht asserts that Adams, with a
"fine intuitive sense" established "with more than
usual brilliance" to both Britain and the Holy
Alliance an area (the Western Hemisphere) that would
be free from their policies (369). It was Adams who
did the "divining, sensing, seizing, adapting, and
combining, at just the right moment in history" to
produce "the most significant of all American state
papers" (Bemis 408).

BIBLIOGRAPHY

Adams, John Quincy. The Adams Chronicles.
    Ed. Jack Shepherd. Boston: Little, 1975.
_____. The Selected Writings of John Adams and
    John Quincy Adams. Ed. Adrienne Koch and William
    Beden. New York: Knopf, 1972.
Bemis, Samuel Flagg. John Quincy Adams and the
    Foundations of American Foreign Policy. New
    York: Knopf, 1949.
Commager, Henry Steele, and Allan Nevins. The
    Pocket History of the United States. New
    York: Pocket, 1951.
Curti, Merle, Williard Thorp, and Carlos Baker.
    American Issues: The Social Record.
    Philadelphia: Lippincott, 1960.
Elkins, Harold. "The Holy Alliance and a Young
    Democracy." American Perspective, 39.2
    (1978): 84-92.
Hecht, Marie B. John Quincy Adams: A Personal
    History of an Independent Man. New York:
    Macmillan, 1972.

14

Hicks, John D. and George E. Mowry.   <u>A Short</u>
     <u>History of American Democracy</u>.   Boston:
     Houghton, 1956.

LaFeber, Walter.   <u>John Quincy Adams and American</u>
     <u>Continental Empire</u>.   New York: Knopf, 1946.

Perkins, Dexter.   <u>Hands Off</u>.   Boston: Little,
     1975.

Russell, Evelyn.   "John Adams as a Politician."
     <u>Southern Historic Review</u>, 22 (1982): 315-324.

INDEX

CORRECTION MARKS FOR PART III
MECHANICS

MARK	FAULT	SECTION
qt	Incorrect use of quotation marks	*1*
ital	Incorrect use of italics	*2*
hyph	Incorrect hyphenation	*3*
cap	Capitalization required	*4*
u-cap	Unnecessary capitalization	*4*
abbv	Error in abbreviation form	*5*
num	Error in use of numbers or figures	*6*
sp	Error in spelling	*7*